How to be an Outstanding Childminder

Second edition

KU-450-833

by Allison Lee

BLOOMSBURY

LONDON • NEW DELHI • NEW YORK • SYDNEY

Published 2013 by Bloomsbury Education
Bloomsbury Publishing Plc
50 Bedford Square, London, WC1B 3DP

www.bloomsbury.com

9781441172853

A CIP record for this publication is available from the British Library.

1 3 5 7 9 10 8 6 4 2

Typeset by Fakenham Prepress Solutions, Norfolk, NR21 8NN
Printed by CPI Group (UK) Ltd, Croydon, CR0 4YY

This book is produced using paper that is made from wood grown in managed,
sustainable forests. It is natural, renewable and recyclable. The logging and
manufacturing processes conform to the environmental regulations of the
country of origin.

To view more of our titles please visit www.bloomsbury.com

Contents

Acknowledgements

I have been privileged to work with a vast number of families over the past 20 years that I have been a childcare practitioner and I would like to thank all of these for allowing me to be a part of their child's care and development.

Special thanks to Chris and Vicki Green for giving me permission to use photographs of their son, Reece, in this book.

Introduction

So, you want to be an outstanding childminder? You want to achieve the status and stay there? You are itching to hang the certificate on your wall, polish it with pride and show it off to all your customers, past, present and future, to prove that you have achieved the highest possible standards and are intent on continuing to do so. Your aim is to be the best, to show that the service you provide is exemplary and that there is no better childminder for miles around, with the dedication, tenacity and perseverance to reach the standards and stay there. You are not satisfied with being just 'good'; you want to be at the top level of excellence. I cannot profess to have all the answers and indeed it is impossible to second-guess what any one day will reveal, as each and every family you work with will be unique. However, what I can do is share my years of experience of working with children and their families and show you how to dodge the minefield of potential problems so that you can become outstanding in your chosen profession while actually enjoying your work!

I am sure many of you who have purchased this book are already outstanding in practice and that the families you work with are extremely pleased with the service you provide (if they aren't they shouldn't still be with you!), but now it is time to get those Ofsted inspectors on board and to show them what you are capable of so that you can gain the recognition you justly deserve for your hard work and commitment.

If you have bought this book, the chances are you are aiming to achieve an outstanding grade. Your inspection may be imminent or you may just be hoping to gain a little additional information in a particular area. Whatever your reasons for buying this book, I hope that it provides you with the inspiration you are looking for to bring your own childminding business to the highest standard and shows you how to keep it there.

Chapter 1
The Outstanding Childminder... Unleashed

The days of 'minding' children are well and truly over. Childminders are no longer the poorly-paid babysitters of the past. They are now highly professional, qualified individuals running well-respected businesses.

Childminders are no longer paid to 'watch over children'; they are expected to care for them, teach them, entertain them, cook for them, clean for them, supervise them, befriend them and nurse them – so you had better be prepared! Anyone expecting an easy ride will be in for a shock and if you are hoping to achieve an 'outstanding' grade then the ride may be even tougher.

However, each and every one of you has the potential to reach the highest grade for your childminding business and it is hoped, if you are reading this book, that this is your ultimate aim.

So, what is an outstanding childminder? In addition to meeting the Ofsted criteria (www.ofsted.gov.uk) you also need to go that extra mile to create a good relationship with the children and their parents. Childminders are often seen as an extension to the family and this is a wonderful position to be in. It means that not only are you a trusted person to care for children – you are also a friend and confidant. This can, however, cause problems as there is a fine line between staying professional and being a friend.

So what are the roles of the childminder and how can you ensure that you carry them out to the best of your ability?

The carer

While working as a childminder your role will involve being a carer for children. Parents will expect you to care for their children as you would your own. You will have the responsibility of making sure that the children are safe at all times when they are with you and you will be expected to be aware of, and remove, any potential hazards. You will need to know how to comfort a child when they are upset, appease them when they are angry and entertain them when they are bored.

The teacher

It is generally believed that the sooner a child starts with their education the brighter they will be. This is reflected by the training offered to childminders to enhance their skills, and also by the Early Years Foundation Stage.

The hours you work as a childminder and the ages of the children you care for will have a great influence on how you carry out your role as an educator. If you care for pre-school children you will need to be equipped with the necessary knowledge to enable you to promote the statutory framework for the Early Years Foundation Stage. If you provide care for school-aged children it will be useful for you to be aware of the topics being taught in school. It is beneficial to familiarise yourself with the methods currently being taught with regard to how children learn to read and write and how numeracy skills are promoted – these have changed a great deal since most of us were at school!

The entertainer

How do you keep a bored toddler from crying or entertain four eight-year-olds in the school holidays when the typical British weather means that it has rained solidly for three weeks in the summer? You will need to learn fast how to become a great entertainer or you will quickly lose your customers when the children plead with their parents not to go to work because it's 'soooo boring at the childminders!' In today's society of media entertainment and an untold number of electrical gadgets it is not too hard to keep the older children happy for a few hours if the weather is so bad that you are prevented from doing the things you would like to do outdoors. However, although children may be perfectly content playing on the Wii, Xbox or computer, or simply being glued to the television for an afternoon, it may well be that their parents won't share the same sentiments and you may find yourself with some unhappy parents questioning what exactly they are paying you for!

Although it is perfectly acceptable to use the television and games consoles for some of the entertainment, you must not rely on them too much. If the weather is wet, dig out the old favourites like Monopoly, Snakes and Ladders and good old Hangman. Games like these teach children so much more than a PlayStation or Xbox ever could and they are also much less expensive!

Entertainment needs to address all children of all ages and with all preferences, so brush up on your gaming skills. You may need to be an expert at football, cricket, netball, bowling and golf, in addition to being able to play a variety of musical instruments and becoming a master baker.

Entertainment need not be expensive. In addition to trips to the play gym and cinema, consider taking a packed lunch to the woods and making dens – hours of endless fun for children of all ages and it costs next to nothing.

The chef

As a childminder, your role may involve providing meals for the children in your care – breakfast, lunch and/or dinner, depending on the times you are working. As we all know children can be faddy eaters. They may be happy to eat anything you throw at them if this comes in the form of crisps, biscuits, cakes and fizzy drinks; however this is not the kind of menu that parents will be looking for and it most certainly will not gain you an outstanding award from Ofsted! You will, therefore, need to know all about healthy eating. This is not just as simple as knowing how many portions of fruit and vegetables a child should be eating every day – it will also involve knowing how to *disguise* these portions in order to ensure that the children actually eat them!

In order to please both parents and children it is a good idea to ask both to provide a list of their preferences. Although these lists will inevitably vary considerably, with the children's list including pizza, burgers and chips and the parents' including salmon, pasta and homemade vegetable soup, you will at least be in a position to see what the parents' preferences are and what you are likely to get the children to eat, and hopefully an acceptable balance can be found. Homemade pizza, for example, using fresh vegetables, would most likely be an acceptable meal for both parents and children.

It is a good idea to stick to a tried and tested menu and vary this from week to week. If you decide to use a set menu it is important that you rotate your meals and, instead of having a weekly menu, perhaps opt for a fortnightly or monthly cycle to avoid serving the same meals to the same children every week.

Consider printing your menus and displaying them for parents to see. Offer the Ofsted inspector a chance to look at the kind of meals you provide and enrol on a suitable course to help you gain your food hygiene certificate.

The cleaner

Sadly, you will be responsible for cleaning up the mess after the children have left and this can, in many cases, make an already long day even longer. The baking session, which seemed such a good idea only a couple of hours ago and which the children enjoyed immensely, has left your kitchen looking as if a bomb has hit it. You reel at the playdough ground into your carpet and the paint spattered on your walls and wonder if it was all worth the effort. Well, of course it was! The children have had a wonderful day and have gone home with exciting stories to tell their parents with freshly iced cupcakes for supper. So what's a bit of flour on the floor or paint on the walls – everything cleans, right?

Working in your own home can also have an impact on the kind of activities you provide for the children and no parent should expect you to allow children to paint and use glue in your living room. It is, however, your responsibility to provide suitable places for children to carry out these important activities, and careful consideration should be given to the type of surfaces and flooring you have in these areas and the ability to be able to clean them easily. The Ofsted inspector will take everything into consideration when they visit your home and, if your house is immaculate and children are not given the opportunities to play and learn in an adequate manner, you will not gain an outstanding grade. Even the smallest of homes can, with a little careful thought and planning, provide adequate spaces for all the messy play children enjoy and it is up to you, the childminder, to ensure that this is possible. If you do not want your house 'messed up' then you are in the wrong profession and the inspector will very quickly see through any disguise.

The supervisor

Supervising children effectively comes with practice. You need to get to know the children well before you can be really confident of when to sit back and let them 'get on with things' and when to intervene. Allowing children the opportunity to feel they have achieved something for themselves builds their confidence and self-esteem, and it is the childminder's job to know when to offer support and when to allow them to work things out for themselves.

Supervising children's behaviour can be one of the hardest parts of the job. Getting children to behave some of the time is difficult; getting them to behave all of the time is nigh on impossible! So, one of the most important things to bear in mind is that children will misbehave. No child is perfect (regardless of what their parents would like you to believe!) and all children will, at some point, push the boundaries to see how far they are allowed to go.

If I had a pound for every time someone had asked me 'What shall I do if so and so has a tantrum when the Ofsted inspector is here?' then I would be one very wealthy lady! Whether or not little Mary has a tantrum or whether Alfie bites George or Evie pulls Betty's hair is irrelevant – believe me, the inspector will have seen it all! What is important is how you DEAL with the situation: whether you remain calm and address the issue in a suitable manner, or whether you stand in the room tearing your hair out screaming, 'Well, that's it kids – I've failed the inspection now due to your behaviour!!' Hopefully you will know how to deal with the situation correctly and if you choose the second option then, no, you most definitely will not gain an outstanding grade. Being able to deal with children's behaviour is a crucial part of the job and one that you must master if you are to show the inspector how competent you are.

The friend

This is a difficult one but by no means impossible. Despite needing to keep things on a professional level, it is also possible to be good friends with the children you care for and their families and, in many respects, this part of the service is essential. Being 'friends' doesn't have to mean having dinner at each other's houses every week or going on shopping trips together; it simply means having a mutual respect for one another. There is a deep satisfaction in making good friends with the children and their families. Many childminders remain friends with their families for many years to come and have the satisfaction of witnessing the children grow up into adults and even having children of their own.

However, it is important to ensure that by becoming a 'family friend' you are not putting yourself in the position of becoming the 'family mug'. Don't allow the friendship to stop you pointing out if you haven't been paid on time, or if the parents are collecting their children later and later each day resulting in you being made to work unpaid overtime on a regular basis. For a friendship to be genuine it needs to work both ways and you must never allow yourself to be taken advantage of, as this will lead to resentment and dissatisfaction in the job. Outstanding childminders should rarely become dissatisfied!

The nurse

First-aid training is compulsory for all childminders. Gaining suitable training will give you the confidence to deal with first-aid situations; however, it is vital that you know your limitations. A twelve-hour paediatric first-aid course does not put you in the running to become the next brain surgeon! If you are unsure of a child's symptoms, it is vital that you take appropriate advice and act on it.

Childminders are not nurses and your home is not a hospital. If the Ofsted inspector knocks on your door and your home resembles a hospital ward with clearly unwell children, it will not bode well. Children may, of course, be left in your care with a cold; this is perfectly acceptable. However, if they are running a high temperature and vomiting and clearly are not enjoying their time in the setting or being able to take part in the activities, then they should not be there. In cases like these the children pose a threat to the others in your care – and to yourself – and they should be sent home. It is your responsibility to ensure that ALL children are well cared for, and putting another child at risk because you have refused to send home a clearly sick child is not good practice, let alone outstanding practice!

Chapter 2
Outstanding... Relationships

Childminders need to forge good relationships with a number of people, such as the local authority, fellow childminders and other professionals. However, the most important relationships which need to be nurtured and cherished are those with the children, their parents and, if working with a partner or assistant, colleagues.

With the new Early Years Foundation Stage having come into force in September 2012 there is greater emphasis than ever before with regard to strengthening partnerships with parents and professionals and, if this has been a weak point of yours in the past, then it is time to address this important issue now.

In addition to sharing with parents what their child has been doing with you during the day, you will also need to be comfortable discussing the child's development and explaining the compulsory areas of learning. As a childminder it should be relatively easy for you to have regular discussions with the parents of the children you are caring for as you will probably be seeing them when they drop off and collect their children. However, it may be that someone else will do this, such as grandparents, aunties, uncles etc., and if this is the case you must think of other ways to communicate effectively with parents. Never rely on someone else to pass on information, as invariably this will get forgotten or misconstrued. You might like to consider using newsletters or daily diaries to relay important information. Regular parents' evenings, often considered more relevant to school and nursery settings, can be equally beneficial for childminders, as you and the parents can sit down, hopefully without distractions, and discuss any necessary developments. Although it is never a good idea to offer advice to parents when they have not asked for it, it is always nice to be approachable and have the parents turn to you when all else fails.

Without effective relationships it is probably true to say that everything else you do will quickly become ineffective. Parents who do not trust and respect you as a professional will soon become disillusioned with the service offered and take their custom elsewhere.

The golden rules for good relationships are:

- be open and honest
- be respectful
- be helpful whenever possible
- be non-judgemental
- be knowledgeable – both about the child and your duties as a childminder.

Working with another childminder or an assistant

Childminding can at times be a lonely profession. You may find yourself at home for many hours with only very young children for company, particularly in the winter months when the weather is bad and it is not as easy to get out and about with toddlers and babies. If you have been used to working away from the home in the past, getting used to the loneliness and having the responsibility of being your own boss can be rather daunting. You must be organised to run your own business, whatever your profession, and you must take responsibility for things if they go wrong. There is no one immediately at hand to turn to for support, help and advice or to share the workload.

It is for these reasons, together with friendship and companionship, that some childminders opt to work with another childminder or to employ an assistant to work with them. There are, however, both advantages and disadvantages to working with someone else.

Advantages of working with another childminder or employing an assistant

- **Adult company** – Unless you are prepared to take the children you look after to lots of different clubs or outings, which is not always practical as these can be expensive and will have to fit in with your everyday routines, then you will find yourself spending a lot of time without any adult company. Being in the company solely of young children affects people differently and some childminders find it difficult.

- **Sharing views and ideas** – Working alone can result in ideas becoming stale and unadventurous. You may have had lots of ideas for activities at the outset when starting up your business but, after a while, it can be difficult to have the motivation to come up with new ideas to stimulate the children. Having another adult present means that there is the option of 'pooling' ideas. One of you may be brilliant at artwork while the other may have musical ability. By working together you can share your knowledge and expertise, to the benefit of the children.

- **Flexibility and back-up** – If you work alone and you or one of your own children are ill, it can mean letting parents down if you are not able to go about your childminding duties. Working with another childminder or employing an assistant can help overcome this obstacle as there are always two people available. Obviously, you must still adhere to the conditions of your registration and not exceed the number of children *one* of you can care for *alone*.

- **Reassurance** – We all need reassurance sometimes and it is good to have someone there to share the trials and tribulations that running your own business can bring. There may be times when a parent is being unreasonable or is unhappy about a particular situation – hopefully only rarely – and it is always good to be able to seek advice from someone else. It is, of course, important to remember to respect the confidentiality procedures of your setting before discussing certain things with an assistant.

- **Emergencies** – Having another adult present at times of accidents, illnesses or emergencies can be very helpful. It is much easier to stay calm and in control of the situation if you have help readily available. By working as a team it is easier to manage any emergency situation and, should a trip to the hospital be necessary, there is not the added problem of finding someone to look after the other children in your care.

- **Adult:child ratios increased** – By working with another childminder or employing an assistant, the number of children you can be registered to care for is increased. The exact number of children is determined by Ofsted.

- **Shared costs** – Obviously the everyday costs of providing food and drink will not be reduced as you will probably be caring for a larger number of children if you are working with another childminder, but the cost of purchasing toys and equipment should be considerably less as you can share these between you.

Disadvantages of working with another childminder or assistant

- **Authority** – It may be difficult to determine who has the overall authority when important decisions are being made. In the case of working with another childminder disputes could arise, for example, depending on whose house the business is run from. If you employ an assistant you must be confident at giving clear, concise instructions and make sure the assistant is aware of exactly what is expected of them.

- **Differences in work attitude** – Problems may arise if you and the person you are working with have very different attitudes regarding the way you wish to run the business. While one of you may be willing to improve your skills through training courses, the other may not be prepared to give up their free time in this way, and resentment may arise. It must be made clear for everyone involved, prior to starting the business, what is expected from each individual.

- **Friendships** – Friendships may suffer when two people spend long hours together day after day. You may think that you have a solid friendship but tempers can become frayed when faced with the very demanding job of caring for young children.

- **Working out wages, expenses etc.** – It may seem fair to split the profits of the business equally, if you are working with another childminder, and likewise to pay an equal proportion of the cost of purchasing toys, equipment, food and drink; but who is responsible for calculating how much heating, lighting, gas/electricity for cooking, toilet rolls and soap are being used? Who is expected to wash and iron the extra towels and bedding? These are all questions which need to be addressed fairly if your business is to succeed. If you employ an assistant and pay wages you are responsible for Income Tax and National Insurance payments and you must be aware of, and comply with, the employment law in these cases. You are expected to pay your employee the minimum wage (if you feel that they are worth it you might even pay them more!) and as an employer you also need to have employer's Liability Insurance in addition to Public Liability Insurance.

Whether you decide to work alone, employ an assistant or work with another childminder is purely down to preference. What I would recommend though, if you are thinking of working with someone else, is to think very carefully about what you want and how you see your business developing. Work out, in detail, how you are going to calculate your expenditure and organise your accounts. Make sure *all* parties are happy with the arrangements prior to commencing the business and never agree to anything initially that you feel you may resent later on.

Your responsibilities when working with another person

If you do decide to employ an assistant or work with another childminder, it is *your* responsibility to ensure that the person you choose to employ or work with is suitable for the job. In the case of another childminder this may be relatively easy as they will already be registered with Ofsted and, therefore, have undergone the relevant stringent checks. All that is left for you to do is to ensure that you can work with the person and that you have a similar outlook on business matters. If you choose to employ an assistant, then you must do so with caution and ensure that all the relevant checks have been made on them and that references have been followed up *prior* to the commencement of their employment.

When deciding on the suitability of a potential assistant you may find it helpful to use evidence derived from the following to help you to make up your mind:

- **References** – Always ask for references from the candidate's current employer and, more importantly, contact them!

- **Qualifications** – Ask to see the candidate's qualifications. Although holding many qualifications does not necessarily mean that a person is better suited for the job than someone with fewer awards, it does prove their willingness to learn and their competence in studying for and achieving qualifications.

- **Knowledge** – In addition to qualifications, ask what experience and knowledge of children the candidate has.

- **DBS (previously CRB) checks** – Always check that the person is suitable to work with young children.

- **Identity/health checks** – Make sure you are completely satisfied with who the person says they are and that they do not have a health problem which could put them or others at risk in a childminding setting.

- **Employment history** – Ask to see the candidate's employment history and, if they appear to have had numerous jobs, find out why.

- **Interview** – Use the interview to get to know the person. Ask yourself some important questions such as:

  - Could you work with this person?

  - Do you feel the person is capable of working on their own initiative?

  - Is the person approachable?

  - If there are children present, how does the person respond to them and how do they respond to the candidate?

  - Do you feel the person would have a problem taking instructions from you?

Remember you have a duty to inform Ofsted of any changes you make to staffing. This includes whether you decide to work with another childminder or whether you employ an assistant.

Working with parents

Usually parents want the best for their children. How they actually go about achieving this may vary immensely. The important thing to remember is that there are many different ways of successfully bringing up children and many different factors influencing the way parents choose to do this.

Some of the more common factors which can influence the way in which parents may choose to bring up their children are:

- money and employment
- housing
- education
- family structure
- culture
- religion.

Generally speaking parenting styles fall into three main categories. These are as follows.

- **Authoritarian** – This type of parenting tends to be controlling. These parents have many rules in an attempt to manage the behaviour of their children. Quite often authoritarian parents have very high expectations of their children which can often be difficult for the children to achieve.

- **Permissive** – This tends to be the opposite of authoritarian. Permissive parents allow their children the freedom of choice. Often children with permissive parents are more difficult to manage when it comes to behaviour because they have been allowed much more freedom than other children. Although choice and responsibility are good for children, it is also essential that they are not allowed an excessive amount of freedom and it should be remembered that boundaries are essential in order for children to feel safe and secure.

- **Authoritative** – This is the category that most parents fall into. Authoritative parents attempt to manage and control their children's behaviour in a way which enables them to be accepted into society.

They take the time to listen to their children and to explain rules and expectations.

Family structures also have an enormous effect on parenting styles. The main structures are as follows.

The nuclear family – This type of family structure consists of both parents and their children living together and the parents sharing the responsibility of caring for their children.

The extended family – This type of family structure consists of parents, children and relatives all living close by, and sometimes even in the same house, and sharing the responsibility of bringing up the children. Extended family structures were traditional in this country for centuries and are still common practice in many parts of the world.

The single-parent family – This type of family structure consists of one parent living on their own with their children. This type of family occurs when the parents have divorced or separated, when one parent has died or when someone has actively chosen to have children without the support of a partner.

The homosexual/lesbian family – This type of family structure consists of one natural parent living with a partner of the same sex, along with their children.

The reconstituted family – This type of family structure consists of one natural parent and one step-parent living together with the children.

The adoptive family – This type of family structure consists of children who are not living with one or both of their natural parents. Sometimes the children may be unaware that they are adopted and therefore appear to be part of a *nuclear* family structure.

Your responsibilities to parents

Parents, and indeed their children, require different things from childcare and it is the responsibility of the childminder to accommodate their wishes as much as possible. Influencing factors could well be the age and stage of development of the children. Generally speaking parents are looking for childcare which offers their children the chance to be in a stimulating, safe environment. Additional factors they may be looking for are:

- a loving, caring environment
- a chance for their children to mix with others of the same or similar age
- a chance for their children to build their confidence
- a start to their children's education
- a variety of experiences
- an established routine to which their children can relate.

Safety

It is probably true to say that most parents looking for childcare are interested in the safety of the environment and the opportunities and experiences the childminder can offer their children. Safety is a very important part of a childminder's job and you have a responsibility to ensure that the children in your care are safe at all times. In order to do this, it is essential that you look closely at all the indoor and outdoor areas you use for your childminding business and scrutinise every aspect of safety.

Pay special attention to the following:

- **Equipment** – Make regular checks to ensure that there are no worn or broken parts and replace or repair when necessary.
- **Toys** – Make regular checks to ensure that there are no missing or broken parts and replace or repair when necessary.
- **Dangerous items** – Think carefully about how you store knives, medicines, matches, cleaning fluids, alcohol, plastic bags, etc.
- **Electrical items** – Fit locks to fridges, freezers, washing machines, etc., and ensure that flexes from toasters, irons and kettles are not left trailing over work surfaces.
- **Stair gates** – These should be fitted to both the top and bottom of the stairs.
- **Fires** – Guards should be securely fitted around the whole of the fire and its surround.

- **Radiators** – Ensure that these are not too hot when touched and, if necessary, fit covers on them.

- **Electrical sockets** – These should be covered.

- **Food** – It is essential that you practise safe and hygienic work methods when storing, preparing and cooking food.

- **Pets** – Ensure that pets are not allowed on tables or work surfaces and that their feeding bowls, toys and litter trays are not accessible to children. Pets should be routinely vaccinated and treated appropriately for worms and fleas.

- **Smoke alarms** – These should be fitted and working; check batteries regularly.

- **Fire blankets/extinguishers** – These should be in good working order and easily accessible.

- **Nappies** – Hygienic practices must be followed with regard to the changing and disposing of nappies.

- **Bedding/towels** – Each child should be provided with their own clean bedding, towels, flannels or sponges.

- **Low-level glass** – Ensure that the glass in windows, doors, coffee tables, greenhouses, etc. conforms to safety standards.

- **Windows** – These should be fitted with safety catches and no furniture should be placed directly underneath which children can climb on.

- **Banisters/railings** – Check that these are safe and secure and that they do not have spaces where a child could trap their hands, feet or head.

- **Tablecloths** – Ensure that these are not left trailing.

- **Rugs/carpets** – Ensure that no one can trip over rugs or worn/ frayed carpets.

- **Gardens** – Children must not be allowed access to ponds, water butts, sheds, greenhouses, streams, wells, pools, fountains, garages, etc. Poisonous plants must be removed from the garden area accessible to the children, and gates and fences must be checked regularly to ensure they are secure. All dangerous items such as garden equipment must be securely locked away and outdoor toys and equipment must be checked regularly for signs of wear and tear. Pets must not be exercised in the garden area used for childminding purposes.

Why parents choose childminders

Parents who choose a childminder over a nursery setting for their children will do so for a number of reasons. Although some nurseries offer excellent opportunities for children, childminders come into their own for several reasons as they can offer children:

- **Smaller groups** – Most childminders are registered to care for three children under the age of five years and can therefore offer a much more personal service.

- **The same carer** – Being cared for by the same person every day has many benefits for a child and is often preferential to having to get used to several carers in a nursery setting. This can be particularly beneficial to a child who finds new situations difficult to handle.

- **Continuity of care** – Childminders often care for children from several weeks old right through their school years. This is something that nurseries cannot offer and alternative childcare often has to be found once children begin school.

- **Friendship to the family** – Childminders often become an extension of the children's family and excellent friendships may be forged.

- **Better knowledge and understanding** – Childminders often have a better understanding of the children as they are usually the only people, other than the parents, who are caring for the children and they are, therefore, in an excellent position to spot any changes in behaviour and well-being early on.

Dealing with problems

Today's working parents lead busy, stressful lives and although it is true to say that most childminders also lead hectic lives and work long hours, this is often forgotten when a problem arises as people tend to see things only from their own point of view. When dealing with any type of complaint it is important to remember to:

- stay calm
- listen to what the parents have to say
- not interrupt when someone else is telling you something
- get your own message across without resorting to apportioning blame
- refrain from shouting or becoming aggressive.

Problems can and will occur from time to time and it is important to remember that, without accepting the blame for every little thing that may go wrong, you are responsible for ensuring the smooth running of your business. Dealing with any complaints effectively is all part of your job. Some parents can be unreasonable; but, by writing and maintaining appropriate contracts and policies, you should be well on the way to eliminating many of the common problems immediately. Childminding is a *partnership* and it is up to you to ensure that this partnership runs smoothly.

Many of the problems which usually occur are due to misunderstandings and this is where a watertight contract comes into its own (more about contracts in Chapter Five). Always take the time to word your contracts accurately and explain them to parents before inviting them to sign. Make sure that they fully understand what is expected of them and what they in return can expect from you.

Your policies and procedures also go a long way to ensuring that misunderstandings do not occur and you should think carefully about what you are asking of the parents and their children (more about policies in Chapter Five).

Some of the more common problems which may arise include:

- **Behaviour** – Often your own rules regarding behaviour may differ from those of the children's parents. However, it is important to remember that rules have to be made and kept in order for all the children in your setting to be happy and enjoy their time with you. It must be made clear that you expect all the children to abide by your rules *regardless* of what they are allowed to do at home.

- **Payment** – Problems can sometimes arise when parents become lax with their payments and fail to pay on time. These problems can easily be rectified by reminding parents of the contract you have with them and, if necessary, incorporating an additional fee into the contract for late payment. You will find that parents are unhappy paying extra and will ensure that they pay on time once you have exercised your rights to a late-payment fee.

- **Dietary requirements** – Ideally these issues will be discussed and agreed early on, before children take up a place with you. You must always seek the preference of parents where sweets, sugary snacks and fizzy drinks are concerned. Ideally these should be kept to a minimum regardless of parental preference; but you must never give children any of these if their parents have specifically requested you not to.

- **Holidays** – Like payments, this should be discussed and agreed prior to signing the contact. Often parents who have been happy to accept that you will have five weeks' holiday a year are less quick to accept this if your dates are different from theirs and they need to find alternative cover for the time you are away. This problem can be avoided by liaising with the parents about holiday dates and, where possible, giving them lots of notice. Alternatively, plan your holidays together so that your dates coincide.

No matter how hard you work, how many hours you devote to your business, or how dedicated you are to your job, you will almost certainly receive a complaint at some point in your career.

Even childminders deemed outstanding by Ofsted undoubtedly face their share of problems! This is because all families are unique and will not agree with everything you do and say all of the time. As the saying goes: *'You cannot please all of the people all of the time'*. However, you should be striving to *'please most of the people most of the time'*. If you take the time to listen to parents and accept that everyone is different and will have different opinions and values, then you will be well on the way to dealing with any potential problems should they arise.

If you are unfortunate enough to receive a complaint try to resolve the problem as amicably as possible. This is necessary both from a business point of view and from the child's point of view. Children can very quickly detect any animosity between their parents and their childminder and they will become upset and confused if their main carers are at loggerheads.

Encourage parents to meet with you, after work hours when interruptions are at a minimum, to discuss the problem. Allow them to put their point of view across, listen to them without interrupting and take on board what they are saying. After they have had their say, put your own point of view across in a calm and reasonable manner. Do not blame anyone, accept that there has been a difference of opinion and seek to resolve the matter.

When you are communicating with parents it is essential that you treat them as equals. Although it is important to get your own message across, it is equally important to listen to, value and respect the views of the parents in order to establish a friendly relationship based on trust and mutual understanding. A poor relationship with the child's parents will inevitably cause problems in the long run.

Working with children

Unlike parents, children are relatively easy to keep happy! They will not make any unreasonable demands on you and will not expect you to perform miracles. Children are usually happy and content if they feel safe, valued and are offered appropriate activities to stimulate their minds. It is of course your duty as a childminder to enhance this and encourage them to achieve their full potential and ensure that they feel loved and welcomed.

In order for Ofsted to make their judgment about the overall quality of your childminding setting, the inspector will ask the very important question: *What is it like for a child here?* The inspector will judge how well you meet a series of outcomes for children. These outcomes are as follows:

- How do you help children to be healthy?

- How do you protect children from harm or neglect and help them to stay safe?

- How do you help children to enjoy themselves and achieve their full potential?

- How do you help children to make a positive contribution to your setting and to the wider community?

- How do you help children to achieve economic well-being?

Your responsibilities to children

Children have five basic needs, which are illustrated in the diagram below. It is, of course, expected that all childminders provide for all needs, as the very basis of their work.

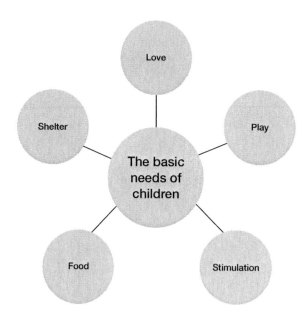

Children's rights

In addition to meeting the children's needs, all childminders need to be aware of children's rights and ensure these are kept to. All children have the right to:

- survival
- protection from harm, abuse and exploitation
- develop to their full potential
- participate fully in social, cultural and family life
- express their views
- have their views listened to, valued and taken into account
- play, rest and enjoy their lives.

The basic human rights of children entitle them to things such as food, healthcare and protection from abuse. However a child's rights are different from those of an adult as children cannot always stand up for themselves. Children need a special set of rights which take into account their vulnerability and which ensure that adults take responsibility for their protection, stimulation and development. The UN Convention on the Rights of the Child is an international treaty which applies to all children and young people under the age of 18 years. It consists of 54 agreed articles. The treaty outlines the basic human rights of *all* children *everywhere*. Almost every country in the world has agreed to and signed this very important treaty underlying its importance.

There are some rights outlined in the UN Convention which relate particularly to childcare and education and it is these rights of the child that childminders should be most concerned with. The rights which affect childcare are as follows:

- Children have the right to sufficient food and clean water for their needs.
- Children have the right to appropriate healthcare and medicines.
- Children have the right to be with their family or those who will care for them best.
- Children have the right to play.
- Children have the right to be safe and free from harm and neglect.
- Children have the right to free education.
- Children should not be exploited as cheap labour or soldiers.
- Children have the right to an adequate standard of living.
- Disabled children have the right to special care and training.

In addition, there are certain Acts of Parliament which exist and are in place to promote the equality of opportunity and to prevent discrimination. The Acts include the Children Act 1989 which requires that the regulatory body has a set of policies in practice for equality of opportunity and that these policies are reviewed regularly. All childcare practitioners should receive regular updates relating to equal opportunities and they should be provided with details of any relevant training as and when necessary. The Children Act 1989 acknowledges the importance of the child's wishes and opinions.

The Act emphasises the need for parents and carers to be *responsible* for their children rather than to have *rights over* them.

When children first arrive at your setting

It is probably true to say that the most difficult time for a childminder to keep children happy is when they are new to the setting and are missing their parents. This is particularly true for young children who have been with their mother from birth and who may now need a childminder in order for their mother to return to work. You will not be able to take the place of the children's mother while they are in your setting, and you should not be striving to do this. It is your job to reassure the children, offer appropriate activities and comfort them when they are upset.

You will have to adjust your usual routine to cater for new children and to offer additional support until they have settled into your setting. In some ways it is easier to settle a young baby into your setting than an older child. However, when they get to the age of around eight months, babies start to become aware of strangers and may well go through a phase of 'missing mummy or daddy'. Babies of this age can often become upset when being left and it is wise to prepare parents for this possibility. Likewise, the parents may be very likely to miss their baby and may also need your support and reassurance.

Ideally before children start their placement with you, you will have had the opportunity to meet them on several occasions. You may decide to arrange to visit them in their own home and to get to know them on 'familiar territory' or you may prefer to arrange short visits at your own house so that the children can get used to their new setting. You may even decide on a mixture of both. It is important to discuss with the parents which strategy they feel will work best for their child.

Prior to a baby or child starting in your care, you will need to gather as much information about them from their parents as possible, in order to prepare yourself for the task ahead. The more information you have about a child, their likes, dislikes, fears and anxieties, the more equipped you will be to deal with any scenarios thrown at you.

It is important to remember that parents may feel equally anxious as their children – sometimes even more so. They may have feelings of guilt about leaving their children. Reassure them that these feelings are all perfectly normal and offer them the support they need.

Tips for settling children into your childminding setting

- Arrange short visits, prior to the placement commencing, in order to allow the children time to get to know their surroundings.

- Encourage parents to stay with their children for a while, particularly during the first few days, if this is possible.

- Offer support and encouragement to both the children and their parents.

- Encourage children to bring a special toy or comforter from home.

- Avoid forcing children to join in activities or games. If they prefer to sit and watch for a while, allow them to do this and to mix only when they are ready.

- Offer cuddles and reassurance if children become distressed. Remember to allow the children to take the lead on this level and never force children to sit with you and be cuddled if they do not want to do so.

- Offer simple, straightforward activities immediately after parents leave to take their minds off the separation. Ideally you will have discovered what particular activities the children prefer and you will be able to offer these. Avoid anything which requires a lot of concentration.

Once parents have decided they are going, encourage them to do just that! Long-drawn-out goodbyes are not a good idea, and can be stressful for everyone. Encourage the parents to establish a routine for saying goodbye and to stick to it. Children may become very upset if the departure is delayed, and a child who is not crying at the start of the farewell may well be hysterical by the time it has finished! Always encourage parents to actually say goodbye and kiss their children. *Never* allow them to 'sneak' off without telling their children they are going. This may result in children becoming clingy as they will come to expect their parents to 'disappear'. If children do not understand where their parents have gone they may suffer unnecessary distress and become distrustful.

On the following page is a routine which you may like to encourage parents to follow when saying goodbye to their children, particularly in the early stages of the placement when the children are still settling into your setting.

- Parent and child arrive at your house.

- Greet both the parent and child warmly as they come in.

- Either you or the parent takes the child's coat off.

- Ideally, in the case of an older child, you will already have a suitable activity prepared and you should then tell them about it.

- Prior to the child commencing the activity, encourage them to kiss their parent and say goodbye.

- Encourage the parent to tell their child that they are going and that they will be back at lunchtime/teatime, etc.

- Allow the parent and child to say goodbye in their own way.

- Parent leaves.

Chapter 3
Outstanding... Observations

Before you can begin to assess a child and plan for their learning and development, you need to know how to observe them. Observations are vital for childminders to find out what stage a child is currently at, what their needs are and what interests them. Without knowing how to successfully observe a child, the assessment and overall planning in the setting will be greatly affected.

The Early Years Foundation Stage

In September 2012 the Early Years Foundation Stage (EYFS) framework changed. The reformed EYFS takes forward the Government's changes to the 2008 framework as recommended by the 2011 Tickell Review.

Two of these reforms are that practitioners must:

- focus on the three prime areas of learning most essential for children's readiness for future learning and healthy development, and
- introduce a progress check at the age of two years.

Prior to the reforms, the EYFS set out six areas of learning; since September 2012 these have been increased to seven but split into three 'prime areas of learning' and four 'specific areas of development'.

Prime areas of learning

- Personal, Social and Emotional Development
- Communication and Language
- Physical Development.

These three areas have been selected as they reflect the beginning of child development and are seen as being crucial to influencing later success in life and learning.

Specific areas of development

- Literacy
- Mathematics
- Understanding the World
- Expressive Arts and Design

These four areas have close links with the National Curriculum.

Another reform of the EYFS is the reduction in the number of 'early learning goals' which was previously 69 and is now 17.

The reformed EYFS now places much more emphasis on how children learn and the focus of effective learning is for children to be 'active'. For children to learn effectively they need to be:

- **Engaged** – Children need to be involved in learning. They should be allowed to explore and experiment.

- **Motivated** – Children need to be encouraged to enjoy achieving what they set out to do.

- **Thinking** – Children should be encouraged to have their own ideas, make links and have choices.

It has been established that the best outcomes for children occur when the activities on offer throughout the day encourage a mixture of child-initiated play and focused learning.

So, what do the terms 'child-initiated play' and 'focused learning' actually mean and how can you ensure that you strike the correct balance?

Child-initiated play and focused learning

It is fair to say that children learn best when they are enjoying what they do. You can probably think back to your days in school when your most preferred subjects were those where you actually 'enjoyed' what was being taught. I, for one, certainly hated my maths lessons – not only did I find the teacher unapproachable, I never enjoyed my time in class when studying this subject. I found the lessons difficult, uninvolved, highly structured and, dare I say it, boring! From my own experiences many years ago, I still firmly believe that a child who is bored will not learn, just in the same way as one who is not involved or allowed to experiment and make choices will be unwilling to learn.

If play and learning are split into four categories, it is much easier to see which categories allow for the best outcomes for children's learning and achievement.

Unstructured play –This is play which does not involve any adult support. Unstructured play should be kept to a minimum.

Child-initiated play – This is play which is actively supported by an adult. Children are allowed to have ideas, make decisions, explore and be involved with the sensitive support and interaction of an adult.

Focused learning – This is play which is guided by an adult. It offers playful experiential activities.

Highly structured learning – This involves very little play. It is highly structured adult-directed learning and, as with unstructured play, it should be kept to a minimum.

It is not difficult to see which categories of play and learning are most suited to children and, ideally, you should be promoting the best outcomes for children's learning through a mixture of child-initiated and focused learning with limited unstructured and highly structured play. By concentrating on child-initiated and focused learning you are able to observe the children while they are engaged in independent learning.

Observations and assessments

Before it is possible to understand fully how to carry out an observation or an assessment, it is important first to understand what is really meant by 'observation' and 'assessment'.

Observation

Observation involves the gathering of information about a particular child's behaviour and their stage of development.

It is necessary to seek parental approval before carrying out an observation of a child. When seeking parental approval you need to inform the parents of the following:

1   Why you feel an observation would be beneficial.

2   What you are hoping your observation will achieve or reveal.

3   How you feel the observation will assist you in planning for the child's future needs.

You also need to reassure the parents that you will share the information from the observation with them and that all the details will remain confidential and will be accessed only by them, yourself and any other professionals on a 'need-to-know basis'. Always point out to the parents that the reason for an observation is to focus on the *positive* aspects of the child's behaviour and progress, rather than looking to produce a *negative* list of underachievement.

Observing a child means that you are watching and studying what they do. You will be observing children all the time while they are in your care to make sure they are safe, to make sure they have the appropriate toys and equipment to play with, and to see whether they are tired or hungry or whether they need a nappy change. This kind or observation will come automatically to you as you are a professional person who is knowledgeable about the care of young children and you are aware of their needs and requirements. There are, however, many more reasons why it is necessary for you to observe children such as shown in the diagram on the following page.

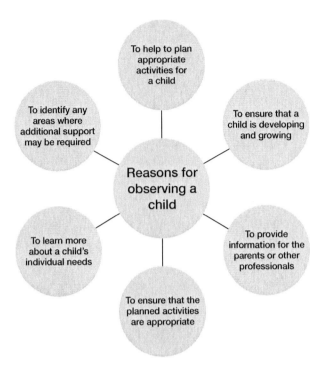

The nature of a childminder's job means that you will be very busy throughout your working day and it is, therefore, necessary for you to choose a method of observing and assessing the children in your care which is easy for you to understand and, more importantly, implement. Try not to see observation and assessment as an additional task but as an essential one which will enable you to be aware of the things the children in your care can do, what they are almost capable of doing and what they need assistance with. Observing and assessing children will not only help you to pinpoint where a child is at in terms of development and growth but it will also help you to identify any problems or concerns.

Methods of observation

There are several methods of observing children and each individual will have their own preference as to which method they prefer. It may be necessary for you to use several methods of observation during the course of your work, depending on whether you require a quick, informal observation or an in-depth account. The figure below shows some of the different ways of observing children.

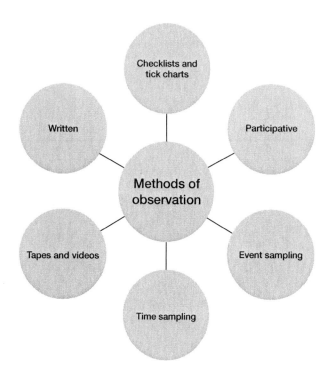

Checklists and tick charts

These can be particularly useful to record what stage a child is at, for example how many colours they can recognise, how many numbers they can count in sequence and whether or not they can recognise the letters of the alphabet. Checklists and tick charts are quick and simple to use and are particularly helpful at future dates to see how a child has developed and whether there are any changes since the last observation. On the next page is an example of a tick chart.

TICK CHART

Name of child

Age of child

Date

Activity	✗	✓
Able to hold a paintbrush		
Able to hold a pencil		
Able to use scissors to cut paper		
Able to tie a shoelace		
Able to fasten a button		
Able to catch a ball		
Able to throw a ball		
Able to kick a ball		
Able to ride a bicycle		

Obviously the statements you insert in your own tick chart will depend on the age of the child you are observing. For example, if you are using this method to observe a nine-month-old-baby the statements may read something like:

- Able to sit up unaided.
- Able to pull themselves to a standing position.
- Able to roll from front to back.
- Able to roll from back to front.
- Able to clap hands.
- Able to wave goodbye.
- Able to crawl.

The main disadvantage of checklists is that they offer very little additional information.

Participative observations

These are when you yourself actually take part in the activity with the child. The main disadvantage of this type of observation is that it can be difficult for you to write notes and record what is happening at the actual time, and you may, therefore, have to rely heavily on your memory to record your observations at a later date.

Event sampling

This method of observation is often used to record patterns of behaviour. Generally speaking, event sampling is useful to record an area of a child's behaviour which you and the child's parents would ideally like to change, for example, temper tantrums. By recording exactly what happens prior to the child's tantrum, it is possible to spot 'triggers' in behaviour which, if managed correctly, can be eliminated. On the next page is an example of what might be recorded for a child called Sam.

Time sampling

This is another form of event sampling, but this time you observe what the child is doing at fixed intervals throughout the day, for example every hour throughout the whole day or every thirty minutes throughout the afternoon.

Tapes and videos

These are really only beneficial for observing children if they are not aware of their presence. You may find that a child who knows that a video camera is pointing at them will play up and act out of character making your observation unnatural and, therefore, ineffective. A tape recorder may be easier to hide, but the disadvantage here would be background noise if you are caring for several children. If you do choose to use tapes and videos to observe the children in your care, make sure that you always get the written permission of the parents before making any form of recording of their child.

Written observations

Written observations enable the recording of information about a child's growth and development or their behaviour over a short period of time. They require very little planning and preparation and can usually be done quickly at any time.

EVENT SAMPLING SHEET

Name: Sam

Age: 3 years 4 months

Aim: To ascertain what triggers Sam's temper tantrums

Date: 10th July 2012

Times observations took place: 11.35am – 12.30pm

4.15pm – 5.00pm

Event	Time	What happened?	Comments
1.	11.35am	Sam approached a child who was happily playing with the cars and took the toys from him.	Sam had a tantrum – he seems to have difficulty acknowledging that he cannot have toys on demand when someone else is playing with them.
2.	12.10pm	Sam refused to sit at the table for lunch because he wanted to sit where someone else was already sitting.	Sam threw a tantrum.
3.	4.35pm	The parent of another child came to collect them – Sam wanted his mum to collect him.	Sam threw a tantrum because someone else was going home before him.

Tips for effective observation

It is important, when observing children, that the information you gather is accurate. However, you must also be aware of your own limitations and not attempt to give your own diagnosis to a problem or concern. While the information you have gathered and recorded may well be useful, it is the responsibility of other professionals to decide what, if any, additional support may be required.

One of the easiest and quickest ways of observing a child is to carry out short observations at regular intervals. Depending on the number of children you are caring for, a short observation can be done daily or weekly. Short observations can be very beneficial if a photograph and short caption is included.

This photograph clearly shows how the child is enjoying his surroundings and is experimenting with water and bamboo pipes.

A child enjoys experimenting with water and bamboo pipes

The observation could be linked to both the prime area of learning, 'physical development', and the specific area of development, 'understanding the world'.

All the areas of development can be covered with the use of photographs and, when used with descriptive captions, these are excellent ways of observing children.

This picture shows a child clearly engaging in literacy. A caption for this photograph could confirm that the child holds his pencil in his right hand and has accurate control. Depending on what has been observed, the caption could also explain how well the child could engage in mark-making. His finished piece of work could be saved in his development file along with the photograph and short observation.

A child learns mark-making

Types of observation

As well as *methods of observation*, there are also *types*. The main types of observation are as follows:

- naturalistic
- structured
- longitudinal
- snapshot.

Naturalistic

This is so called because it is an observation which takes place in the child's usual surroundings. The observation allows the child to carry out tasks which they would normally do, without any structuring being attempted by you, the observer.

Structured

This type of observation is the opposite of naturalistic in that the childminder has intentionally set up a particular activity in order to observe how a child carries out a specific task. For example, an obstacle course could be created to observe a child's balance and coordination, or a painting activity to observe a child's fine motor skills.

Longitudinal

When you have settled into a pattern of regularly observing the children in your care and recording your findings, you will build up your own longitudinal records of observation as your findings will show how the children in your care change and progress over a lengthy period of time. Each child's set of records and observations will be their *longitudinal* record which will enable the important adults in their lives namely you, their childminder, and their parents to identify the important milestones and achievements in their lives.

Snapshot

As the name suggests, this type of observation involves trying to achieve a 'snapshot' of how a child is behaving at any given period of time. For example, a snapshot observation of how a child reacts immediately after their parent has dropped them off may be helpful in trying to deal with a child who is clingy and difficult to settle.

Getting the best results from your observations

With all observations there is a certain amount of essential information which must be included such as:

- the name of the child
- the age of the child
- the date and time that the observation was carried out
- the activity the child was involved in during the time the observation took place
- the number, ages and gender of any other children involved in the activity
- the name of the person carrying out the observation.

When carrying out an observation of a child, using whichever method you are most comfortable with and which is appropriate for the purpose it is intended, it is vital that you remember that the observation must be accurate and unbiased. Refrain from adding or taking away findings which you feel may upset or worry parents, as these may be vital clues to the overall assessment of the child. For example, if you are observing a child's behaviour in order to develop an appropriate strategy to deal with tantrums, and you omit the fact that, during an observation, the child lashed out or threw a toy across the room, simply to avoid embarrassing the child's parents, then you risk jeopardising the whole exercise as this is an important part of the child's behaviour which needs to be addressed. Never exaggerate the situation or problem to make it appear worse than it really is. Your observations must be accurate and up to date to have any benefit whatsoever for the child's overall development.

The observations you have carried out will put you in good stead when deciding on how to plan for the needs of the children in your care. For example, your observations and assessments will enable you to:

- see which activities the children enjoy the most
- see which activities the children are least interested in
- determine which activities children are good at
- decide how to extend the activity in order to stretch the skills of the children

- check the children's progress and growth.

The more information you have about the children in your care the better equipped you should be to provide for their needs. Always take your cue from the children and never try to overstretch them before they are ready. When you have found an activity which a child enjoys, introduce it as often as they wish but refrain from extending it until they are competent enough to cope with more complexity.

If you try to push a child too far too soon you risk alienating them, and their self-confidence may even suffer as a result if they feel they have failed in a particular task. For example, a child of two who has just discovered the joy of painting, by using a variety of finger-paints, paint pads and sponges, should be allowed to experiment in this way before you introduce more complex materials, such as brushes, scrapers, stamps and string. Avoid the temptation to indulge them with too many varied and complex materials before they are ready and always be realistic with your expectations.

Likewise, there is little point in planning an activity involving making a collage with a child who cannot yet use scissors correctly. Instead, allow the child the time to practise using scissors on a regular basis and then, when they are confident with this task, introduce making a simple collage.

Assessment

Assessment is your own unbiased, objective reflection of the information you have gathered during your observation. Before finalising your assessment, you should discuss your observational findings with the children's parents and, if necessary, any other professionals, in order for them to add their own comments, opinions and ideas. The results of your assessment should form an essential part of your future planning and they should be used to monitor the children's progress. The diagram on the next page shows the reasons for completing assessments.

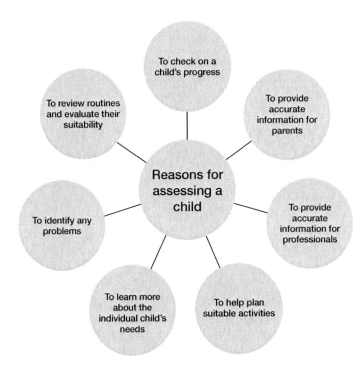

There is little point in carrying out observations on the children in your care if, after doing these observations, you do not assess your findings. As a childminder you will have the advantage of knowing the children in your care well and be in a position to work with them closely on a daily basis. This closeness will enable you to see how the children are growing and developing. By using your observations you will be able to assess the point each child is at and you will then be able to plan appropriate routines and activities to suit each individual child. You need to be aware of the need for your routines to be changed as the children you are caring for grow and develop, and your observations will enable you to see easily when a child is ready to move on to a more complex activity.

Providing reviews

The reformed EYFS has made it compulsory for all practitioners to provide a review of children's progress when they reach two years of age. A short written assessment must be provided for parents or carers which highlights their children's achievements and areas in which extra support might be needed. The assessment must also demonstrate how the provider will address any issues which have been brought to light. It is hoped that this new progress check for two-year-olds will support 'early intervention' and address any need for additional support at the earliest possible opportunity.

Although it is only compulsory for practitioners to provide summative assessments at age two and again prior to the children starting school when the transition forms are completed (more about this in Chapter Nine), it is good practice, and certainly for those who wish to become and remain outstanding practitioners, to carry out regular assessments on the children in their care. Ideally, progress checks should be done periodically, say every six months or so. I would suggest that a child entering your setting at age six months should have a progress check carried out after the following intervals:

- 6 months – or on entering your setting to ascertain where the child is currently at and to enable you to plan for their future development
- 12 months
- 18 months
- 2 years – assessment is compulsory at this age
- 2½ years
- 3 years
- 3½ years
- 4 years – assessment is compulsory along with transition forms at this age.

By assessing the children in your care on a regular basis, rather than simply at the two-year and four-year intervals, it will be much easier to check on each child's progress. You can then be aware of what they have achieved and be effective in planning future needs, as well as highlighting any areas in which the child may require additional support.

It is very important to remember that we do not carry out assessments on children in order to 'label' them. Assessments are required in order that we can ascertain how best to meet a child's needs and help them to progress and achieve their full potential. Although difficult at times, you must not be tempted to 'compare' children. Each child should be seen as an individual and as such they will develop and progress at their own pace rather than at a pace expected of them. A good practitioner will bear this in mind at all times when carrying out observations and assessments of children in their care.

Assessments should be carried out periodically. It is a requirement that assessments must be carried out on a child by the age of two years and again at the age of four when the child is due to begin formal schooling. However, it is good practice to set aside regular times for assessing children a minimum of every six months, enabling you to build up a true picture of the child, to see their current stage and what areas of their development need addressing.

Building a summative assessment

A summative assessment is a short, written summary on the child's progress which highlights the child's strengths and identifies any current weaknesses. A summative assessment needs to cover all seven areas of learning and should include the characteristics of effective learning.

Chapter 4
Outstanding... Planning and Evaluation

Planning is an integral part of a successful childminding business. Although there is no right or wrong way to plan, the method you choose must be easy for you to implement and must take into account the specific individual needs of each child in your care.

If you sit and think about the number of plans you make on a daily basis you would probably be amazed at your findings. Everyone makes plans every day. These plans may not be written down, but everyday lives are based on short- and long-term plans. Important events, such as a wedding or birthday party, are often planned well in advance with lists of things to do, guests to invite and outfits to wear. Everyday routines such as shopping trips and cooking meals are also planned. Before you can begin to bake a cake, for example, you need to check that you have the right ingredients and make a list of what you need to buy.

Of course, not all of the plans you make everyday are methodical in this way. You may start your day mentally planning what you are about to do: get up, have a shower, get dressed, eat breakfast, fill the dishwasher, make the bed, and so on. Then, something happens and your plans must alter slightly to accommodate the change.

It is also important to remember that not all planning results in endless paperwork. Planning can be effective when it is done informally, and experienced childminders are usually planning instinctively with great success.

Planning the day

A large part of a childminder's day may be taken up with school, nursery and playgroup runs, nappy changing and feeding. However, the times in between need to be planned carefully in order to enable the childminder to put some structure into their day and for the children to benefit from suitable activities and experiences, rather than to spend the day being ferried about, fed and changed with little or no quality time for playing and learning.

It is important that you know how to plan your day so that the activities you offer the children enable them to experience variation, in order for them to benefit from their time in your setting. Planning the day also allows you to ensure that there is sufficient time to carry out your intended activities so that the children are able to gain the most from the experience. For example, there is little point in deciding to have a baking session with the children at 3.00pm if you have to leave to collect a child from school at 3.20pm. The activity will either be rushed or abandoned, both of which will be of no benefit to the children. In order for this activity to be a success and for the children to enjoy and learn from it, you need to plan sufficient time to bake, including considering how long it will take to weigh and mix the ingredients, how long the ingredients will take to cook and how long it will take to clear away and wash up, as these are all necessary aspects of the task.

The planning cycle

Although planning is vital when considering children's individual needs, it is also important to understand the whole of the planning *cycle,* including being able to implement the plans and decide whether they are suitable for the children.

As a childminder you need to:

- **Plan** – Think carefully about the children in your care: their ages, their abilities and their preferences. What type of activities do you consider to be beneficial for them? There is little point in preparing to bake a cake if the children you are caring for are too young to help. Likewise, providing baby toys and rattles for a three-year-old will not be beneficial.

- **Implement** – Think carefully about the activities you have planned and decide on the best time for the children to take part in each. Make sure there is sufficient time for the children to actively take part without rushing them. Try to avoid planning complex activities at a time of the day when the children are likely to be too tired to enjoy them.

- **Observe and assess** – There is little point in planning and implementing any activity if you are unfamiliar with how to observe and assess the children to ensure that the activities are suitable. Is the activity too hard or too easy? Do the children appear to be enjoying what they are doing? Are they actively involved? Are they bored?

- **Evaluate** – Finally, after observing and assessing the children while they are taking part in the activity you have planned, you should be able to decide whether the activity has been a success or not. Can the activity be expanded upon? Would you consider repeating the activity? If not, why not? Can the activity be improved?

Planning to make learning fun

One of the responsibilities of a childminder is to provide the children in their care with the best start to their early education. This can be done by giving careful thought to the activities on offer which will give the children a head start in learning while having fun. These early positive experiences will follow through to the children's formal school years.

One of the main reasons parents choose a childminder to care for their children, over a nursery, is that a childminder can offer everyday learning experiences in the home setting, which educates children in an enjoyable way. For example, simple tasks can promote early literacy, such as: sorting the laundry – pairing socks and sorting colours, and setting the table – counting how many knives, forks and spoons are needed. Not only do these tasks encourage children's early education, they do so while helping them to develop in every way rather than in the formal setting of a nursery or classroom.

So, as you make your plans for the day, and consider which activities are suitable for the children in your care, always include a good variety of activities – those that enable the children to begin to learn while at the same time having fun.

Writing plans

Although not all planning needs to be written down, it is an essential part of a childminder's work to be able to provide evidence of their planning during their Ofsted inspection. Therefore, it is necessary for you to get into the practice of writing down your plans. By building up a collection of planned activities and recording and evaluating them, you will be able to refer to them in the future.

Planning is very personal. No two childminders will plan their play and learning opportunities in the same way, quite simply because each childminder is unique and they will be caring for children who are also unique. The abilities and needs of each child may differ enormously and effective planning will take into account each child's personal requirements. There is no right or wrong way to plan your activities, providing the method you choose is effective.

Writing and implementing curriculum plans

It is important to understand the difference between short-, medium- and long-term plans in order to understand how to plan your work. Initially you will need to work out, with the children's parents, exactly what you are hoping to achieve with the planned activity. For example, you could be trying to teach the children how to recognise the three primary colours. Your final goal will be to get them to recognise these colours. However, before reaching this long-term goal, you will have set the children a short-term and medium-term goal, which they will achieve first. You will need to decide on a time frame for achieving each of the goals, the length of which will be dependent on the complexity of what you are hoping the children will learn. A short-term plan may cover a week, a medium-term plan a month and finally, after six months, the children may have achieved the long-term goal.

Some childminders find it easier to plan their activities around a theme or topic, tailored to suit the likes and preferences of the children, and you might like to try this. For example, themes and topics could be planned according to the time of the year – spring, summer, autumn or winter – and the children could be encouraged to take part in activities associated with these seasons. These might include making a display for the wall or going on a nature walk (with careful adult supervision, of course), looking for colourful leaves in the autumn or pretty flowers in the summer. Celebrations such as Christmas, Easter, Diwali and the Chinese New Year also provide excellent themes for planning children's learning and play. It is absolutely essential that children's interests are at the heart of *all* planning and you should involve the children as much as possible.

Depending on the age of the children you are caring for, you may also like to introduce topics such as colours, numbers, shapes and telling the time into your everyday planning. It is always important to remember that, although useful, plans should not prevent children from being allowed to play spontaneously, and time should always be allowed for child-initiated play with planned activities interspersed.

The EYFS makes it clear to practitioners that planning for the children in their care should begin with what is already known about the children in the setting. It stands to reason, therefore, that all planning should be based on the stage the children are already at and build from this.

So, as a childminder you should:

- **Collect evidence about the children in your care** – This can be done through observations and by talking with the children's parents, teachers or previous practitioners.

- **Assess the evidence you have** – You need to look at the evidence you have collected about the child and use this to decide what action you need to take.

- **Use the evidence to plan suitable activities and experiences** – With the evidence you have collected you need to plan suitable experiences for play, both inside and outside, allowing for the child to initiate these experiences whenever possible.

- **Effectively implement your plans** – You need to use the environment and resources available to implement the plans you have made, supporting the children where necessary.

- **Evaluate your practice** – You need to critically examine your practice to evaluate whether you have met the needs of all of the children in your setting and decide how you can effectively extend the children's learning experiences.

Short-, medium- and long-term planning

As I have previously mentioned, planning for children's learning and development can be divided into three categories, namely, short-, medium- and long-term.

Short-term planning

Short-term planning is concerned with differentiation and planning for the needs of specific groups and individual children. This type of planning provides the detail of activities, experiences and resources that the childminder has identified through ongoing observations and assessments of the children in their care. Short-term planning can be used for a specific activity or perhaps for a full day or week's activities.

Medium-term planning

Medium-term planning allows the childminder to look at the continuity and progression of the children from one stage in each area of their learning to the next. This type of planning allows for the identification of the concepts, knowledge, attitudes and skills of the children over a specified period of time.

Long-term planning

This type of planning is concerned with the children's entitlement to a broad and balanced curriculum. The areas of learning and development in the EYFS are achieved through long-term planning over an appropriate length of time.

Therefore a childminder, with the aim of helping children to recognise the three primary colours, may create a curriculum plan like the example given on the following page.

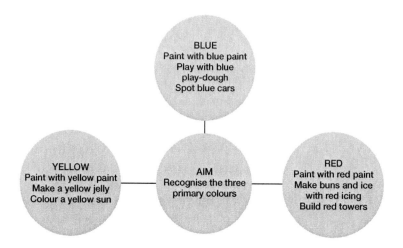

Making sure your plans are effective

When writing curriculum plans for children it is very important that you ask yourself some questions in order to be sure that the plans you intend to implement are both effective and useful.

Before deciding which activities to focus on, consider these questions:

- What activities/experiences/resources will meet the learning outcomes you have in mind for the children?

- Do the activities/experiences/resources support the learning of *all* the children in your care?

- Are the activities/experiences/resources inclusive?

- What are you intending to teach the children?

- Why have you chosen this particular activity/experience/resource?

You then need to think about how you will assess the children while they are taking part in the activity/experience you have planned, including:

- Will you assess the children during or after the activity?

- What method of assessment is most suitable?

- Do you need to save samples of the work?

- Do you need to take photographs?

Finally you will need to evaluate the activity by asking yourself:

- Was the activity/experience a success?
- Were the intended learning outcomes achieved?
- If not, why not?
- What did the children learn?
- What did you learn?
- How could you improve things?
- Do you need to re-evaluate your short- or medium-term plans?
- What other activities/experiences/resources could you provide to encourage the children to achieve the intended learning outcomes?

Planning for mixed age goups

One of the most important, and often difficult, aspects of a childminder's job is being able to successfully plan and provide care and suitable activities and learning experiences for children of mixed age groups. Many childminders will care for children of school age in addition to babies and pre-school children. Although it is true to say that, on most days, the school-age children will be spending the majority of their day away from the child-minding setting while they are in school, it is important to think carefully about how you will provide adequate stimulation and resources for these children both before and after school and during school holidays. Older children should not be expected to take second place and to have their play restricted because of the younger ones, although there may be times when older children will need to consider the ages of the younger ones when requesting certain activities.

Childminders need to carefully consider the toys, books and other resources they provide and make sure that these are suitable for *all* the ages and stages of development of the children they are caring for. For example, eight-year-olds should not be expected to play with baby and toddler toys and teenagers should not have to make do with immature reading material.

All children learn through play and first-hand experiences and it is the duty of the childminder to provide each child with sufficient resources which are appropriate to their age and stage of development in order to provide entertaining and stimulating experiences. Although the way in which the childminder plans their day and the activities they provide influences the way in which the children play and learn, other factors also have an effect, such as the number and ages of the other children in the setting and the amount of quality time the childminder actually spends interacting with them.

Evaluation

Evaluation is the method of judging how much progress the child has actually made over a period of time. Evaluations need to be continuous and systematic and they need to take into account the children's past experiences.

Children are changing all the time and this is why evaluations need to be carried out. As the children grow and progress, you will need to alter your routines and activities to take into account these changes. You will benefit from evaluating not only the children in your care and the activities you provide but also the materials and resources you have on offer and the space and time available.

Evaluations will enable you to:

- encourage the children to concentrate on certain areas of their development
- encourage the children to develop an interest in a variety of areas and activities
- ascertain whether the children are playing well together and if there are any areas of behaviour which are causing concern
- decide whether the toys and equipment available are appropriate for the ages and stages of development the children are currently at and which new toys and equipment may be of benefit
- decide whether any new learning materials will benefit the children

- ascertain whether the activities already enjoyed are stretching the ability and imagination of the children appropriately and whether these need to be assessed.

Evaluating children as individuals

By observing, assessing and evaluating the children in your care you will be able to build up an accurate picture of each child, based on their individuality and preference. Any pre-conceived ideas of what you personally *expect* from each child must be forgotten and you should aim at all times to avoid speculation or allowing yourself to be influenced by prior knowledge. Avoid making comparisons and remember that all children are individuals, unique in every aspect of their make-up, and should be treated with understanding, love and respect.

When evaluating your observations and assessments there may be times when it is apparent to you that something is amiss and that a certain course of action may be necessary. For example, your observations may have revealed a medical problem which may need referral. Always discuss your findings and worries with the child's parents and decide, together, what course of action should be taken. Be sensitive to the feelings of the parents if you suspect their child has some kind of medical problem and take the time to offer support and reassurance. Often something like a hearing impairment is short-lived and may be the result of a particularly heavy cold; however, more severe problems will need ongoing treatment and the parents may feel very vulnerable at this time.

Compulsory reviewing

As previously mentioned in Chapter Three, the reformed Early Years Foundation Stage calls for a compulsory review of a child's progress at the age of two years. Whereas previously no formal assessment at this age was necessary, all practitioners caring for children of this age group will now be required to evaluate their progress in order to highlight achievements and areas on which extra support might be needed – there is more on early identification and intervention in Chapter Six.

Chapter 5
Outstanding... Efficiency and Organisation

Efficiency is paramount in any business. Being methodical and having good systems in place will make for an easier life all round and an outstanding childminder is organised and focused at all times.

Now let's be honest, paperwork is not everyone's idea of fun and, over the years, the main complaints I have heard from childminders, both new and old, is the increasing amount of paperwork the job now appears to entail. I have lost count of the number of times I have heard childminders moan, 'I didn't sign up to mountains of paperwork when I agreed to become a childminder', and 'It's all well and good having to do this paperwork but when am I supposed to play with the children?' The simple truth of the matter is that paperwork is an essential part of childminding, whether we like it or not. In the past, admittedly, paperwork was a lot less, but then the demands on childminders and the shift in professional recognition have also changed and with this change comes responsibility.

By getting to grips early on with the paperwork side of childminding you will be clearing the way for a much easier life later on. Contracts, child record forms, medication forms, etc., all form a necessary part of a childminder's job and you should be efficient in producing and completing all necessary forms and agreements.

Contracts

It is absolutely essential that you have a watertight contract to use in your childminding setting. The contract must be clear and legible with no room for ambiguity. The contract must cover all the main relevant points and must be signed by all parties concerned.

If you decide to draft your own contracts, then it is paramount that you think carefully about what you need to include so that you do not leave anything open to chance, and thereby you will avoid disagreements at a later date.

There are the obvious points which most people will remember to include, such as the days and hours required and the fees payable, but it is also essential that the less obvious things are not overlooked, such as who will be responsible for payment, what the fee includes, who will collect the child, and how much will be charged for late payments or late collections. At the start of a placement it is easy to be trusting and, in an ideal world, everyone would stick to their side of the bargain. However, in reality, this is rarely the case and, should parents start to take advantage of your good nature, it is always easier to rectify problems by referring to the contract as back-up, *providing* you have included all the relevant points.

Begin your childminding relationships with prospective parents in a professional manner. It is likely that you will know very little about the families you work with initially and often discussing topics like fees can be uncomfortable. However, it is important that you overcome these feelings from the start and that you are decisive and confident when negotiating a contract, in order to avoid problems at a later date. A written contract is a condition of a childminder's registration in England and Wales and you should ensure that *all* relevant information is included if you are to protect yourself. Verbal agreements, even with the very best of intentions, will come unstuck at some point.

Most childminders will probably use either specially prepared contracts which can be purchased through organisations such as the Professional Association for Childcare and Early Years (PACEY) or they will produce their own written or computer-generated contracts. It is perfectly acceptable for you to produce your own contracts, providing you are confident at producing such a document and are careful to include all the important points.

Contracts are necessary for several reasons.

- They set out formally what you are willing to do and what you expect from the parents/carers without any misunderstandings.

- They show that you are a professional person working in a businesslike fashion.

- They can be personalised to take into account the differing needs for childcare; for example, a young baby requiring full day care or a seven-year-old requiring before and after school care.

It is important, when completing contracts, that you take the time to sit down with the child's parents or carers and go through each section of the contract with them so that they completely understand what they are agreeing to. Any concerns should be discussed *prior* to anyone signing the contract and these should be cleared up to the satisfaction of everyone involved.

It is important when completing contracts that you do not agree to something which may later have an adverse effect on either the way you carry out your business or the other children in your setting. Be firm and do not allow yourself to be pressurised into agreeing to something which is not practical. Remember the contract is a *mutual* agreement stating what both parties are happy to do.

When you and the parents are both happy with the content of the contract, then sign and date it. You should keep one copy and the parents or carers should retain the other. In the case of involvement with any agencies, such as social services, they would also retain a copy of the contract.

Contracts should be reviewed regularly. It is always a good idea to incorporate a review date on the contract to go through the routine arrangements and to ensure that everyone is still happy with the arrangements. This could be every 6 or 12 months; however, it is also important that the contract is reviewed as soon as any changes are made. For example, if the parent increases their working hours or changes the days they require childcare, then this must be recorded and the contract updated accordingly.

If you decide to create your own contract, it is important that you take the time to think carefully about all the aspects you will need to include such as:

- your full details, including your name, address, telephone number, registration number, insurance details, etc.

- the child's full name, address and date of birth
- the parents' or carers' full names, addresses and contact details
- contracted days and hours
- the fees payable, including whether these fees are payable in advance or in arrears, whether they are payable weekly, monthly or termly, whether they include Bank Holidays, retainers or a deposit
- details of holidays and any payments due during these periods
- details of sickness arrangements and payments due during these periods
- details of any unsociable or overnight care
- details of any charges made for late payment, early drop offs or late collections
- details of who is responsible for paying the fees
- details of who is responsible for paying any additional fees such as pre-school, school clubs or routine outings
- details of what is included in the fee, for example: meals and snacks, nappies, formula milk, toiletries, etc.
- notice of termination required on both sides
- review date of the contract
- details of any special arrangements
- details of any settling in periods
- details of what the parent will be expected to provide for their child, for example: waterproofs in winter if you have to walk the children to school; a comforter or dummy if the child requires these; nappies, formula milk, etc.

There are one or two other things which you may need to consider. However, these are more personal and will only be relevant to some of the families you work with. These might include, for example:

- **Caring for children from the same family** – Are you prepared to offer concessions for siblings? You should think carefully before offering concessions and only do so if you can afford the loss in earnings. Make it clear on your contract that the concession is given to the *oldest* child and that, when they leave the setting, your regular fee will apply to the remaining child.

- **Maternity leave** – If a parent already using your service is expecting a baby, she may wish to keep her older child with her during her maternity period while requesting that you keep a place open for both this child and the new baby. Under these circumstances you would be well advised to terminate the original contract and draw up a new one to cover the period of maternity leave. You may wish to negotiate part-time paid hours for the older child and/or a retainer fee to hold the place. A retainer fee cannot, however, be charged for the baby until after it is born. A new contract should then be negotiated once the mother has returned to work and both her children are in your setting.

- **School holidays** – You may be asked to care for the child of a school teacher. If the parent decides that they wish to keep their child with them during school holidays, then you should negotiate a retainer fee. Think carefully about the drop in earnings and make sure that this is a feasible option for you before agreeing to it.

Record forms and how to complete them

In addition to having a contract, it is essential that childminders draw up an accurate record of all the children in their care. This record should contain details such as:

- the child's full name, address and date of birth

- the address and contact details of the child's parents, including work details

- details of who is authorised to drop the child off and collect them from the childminding setting

- details of the 'password' if one is necessary. Sometimes parents may need to arrange for someone else to collect their child. Ideally you will have already met this person; however, in unavoidable situations this may not be the case. If the child is too young to recognise the person collecting them, then it is a good idea to have a password known only to you, the child's parents and of course the person collecting. If the person collecting does not know the password, *do not* hand the child over to them. Even with a password in place, if you are in any doubt whatsoever about the validity of a person calling to collect a child, do not hand them over. Telephone the parent for confirmation first

- details of the child's general practitioner

- details of any health problems or ongoing medical treatment, such as inhalers for asthma

- details of any immunisations the child has had

- details of the child's likes and dislikes

- details of the child's first language and any other languages they may speak away from the childminding setting.

Medical forms and how to complete them

Before you can give a child any form of medication or injection, or carry out any invasive procedure, you must have the written permission of the child's parents and have undergone any necessary training that enables you to carry out these procedures competently.

Upon signed permission from the parents you will also need to know:

- what the medicine is for and how it should affect the child, so that you will know if it is working

- the exact time the medicine needs to be taken and whether it is necessary to administer before or after meals

- the exact dose required

- when the medication was last given

- the necessary procedure to follow if the medication does not appear to be working

- how you should store the medicine; for example, whether it needs to go in the fridge or be kept at room temperature

- how the medication should be given to the child; for example, orally, using a spoon or syringe, or injected

- whether the medication produces any side effects

- what procedure you should follow in the event that you forget to administer the medicine at the stated time.

As with contracts and record forms, specially prepared medical forms can be purchased from organisations such as PACEY.

Attendance registers

Childminders need to complete an attendance register which sets out the number of children cared for and their ages. The Ofsted inspector will request to see this register when carrying out their inspection.

It is important that you get into the habit of completing your register *regularly*. It is preferable to fill in your register every day when the children arrive at and leave your setting. However, at the very least, you should aim to do this every week. Leaving it any longer will result in you having to rely heavily on your memory and, if you have several children coming and going, it may not be possible to remember the times each child arrived at and departed from your setting.

Attendance registers are very important and they need to be accurate and up to date. Always get the parent to sign their child's attendance record at the end of each week to prove their agreement to the hours their child was in your care. This is particularly useful in the case of an accident or illness when you may need to refer to your attendance record to clarify when the child was in your setting.

Once again, you may like to purchase a pre-printed attendance register from PACEY. However, it is also perfectly acceptable to produce your own. And, if you choose to do this, you may like to consider the example given on the following page.

CHILD'S ATTENDANCE RECORD: WEEKLY

Month: July 2013

Name of child: David

Date of birth of child: 02/01/2011

Week commencing: 2nd July 2013

Day	Time of Arrival	Time of Departure	No. of Hours
Monday	7.45am	5.45pm	10
Tuesday	9.00am	4.00pm	7
Wednesday	9.00am	4.00pm	7
Thursday	9.00am	4.00pm	7
Friday			0
Saturday			0
Sunday			0
Total hours			31 hours

Childminder's signature ....

Parent's signature ....

Accounts

Many self-employed people shudder at the thought of being responsible for their accounts. The key to successful accounting is to do it *regularly*. Keeping up with your accounts by doing little and often is preferable to leaving them for months and then frantically having to search for vital receipts at the end of the tax year.

Like all self-employed people, childminders are responsible for keeping accurate tax and business records, regardless of whether they need to pay income tax or not. You will need to register for tax and National Insurance contributions as a self-employed person and you can do this by visiting www.hmrc.gov.uk or by telephoning HM Revenue and Customs on their helpline number 0300 200 3504.

The accounts you keep must contain details of all the money you receive and spend through your work as a childminder and you must retain these records for six years and you are obliged, by law, to ensure that the records you keep support the figures you enter on your tax return.

ACCOUNTS

ANNUAL COSTS	WEEKLY COSTS
Registration fee payable to Ofsted	Food and drink purchased for the children you are childminding
Public liability and household insurance	Wages for yourself and any assistant you may employ, including NIC and Income Tax
PACEY membership fee (if applicable)	Items such as paper, paints, craft materials, etc.
Training costs for professional development, including first-aid training	Travel expenses incurred while carrying out your childminding duties, such as petrol to take the children to clubs, schools, etc.
Wear and tear on premises and equipment	The cost of activities, outings and treats for the children you are childminding
Increased household bills, including heat, light, water, etc.	Birthday cards and gifts for the children you care for in your childminding work
Equipment and toys	
Christmas presents for the children you care for in your childminding work	

You will need to be aware of what your costs are for running your business before you can successfully decide on how much to charge for your service. It is not a good idea to *guess* at a rate, or to base your fees on the *going rate* for your area, although obviously you will need to take this into consideration in order not to set your fees too high or too low. It is worth bearing in mind the following expenditure when calculating the costs you will incur as a childminder on either a weekly or annual basis.

WEEKLY EXPENDITURE

Week commencing 2nd July 2013

INCOME			EXPENDITURE		
DATE	ITEM	AMOUNT	DATE	ITEM	AMOUNT
02/07/12	Fees – David Sam	75.00 25.00	02/07/12	Food for Children's teas	6.35
09/07/12	Fees – Cathy	15.00	09/07/12	Paper Paint Glitter	4.99 6.50 .99
16/07/12	Fees – Cathy Sam	15.00 25.00	16/07/12	Petrol	25.00
23/07/12	Fees – Cathy Milk Refund	15.00 13.75	23/07/12	Postage to PACEY Toilet rolls Professional carpet clean	.28 4.99 25.00

It is, of course, entirely up to you how you decide to keep your accounts. There is no set way, and it is very much a matter of personal preference. However, what you must make sure is that your records are accurate and up to date. Many people choose to set up their accounts on a personal computer and there are many suitable computer software programs available. However, if you prefer to have handwritten accounts, these too are perfectly acceptable and an accounts book with pre-printed columns can be bought from many high street stores. Accounts books can also be purchased from PACEY and these are straightforward and easy to understand. Your accounts should be neat and accurate so that you can see, at a glance, what you have earned, what you have spent and any profit or loss you have made.

The example shown on the previous page is one way of setting out income and expenditure. The trick is to find a method that works for you and to be disciplined when completing your accounts. Set aside some time, say once a week or once a month, when you can devote yourself to getting your accounts up to date. By being organised you will save yourself a lot of hassle in the long run. Make sure you keep all your receipts and number these. You can then write the number of the receipt next to the item it relates to on your account sheet so that you can see easily which receipt matches which expense. It is a good idea to either staple the receipts to the appropriate page of your accounts or keep them in numerical order in a separate folder.

By adding up the figures in each of the columns headed 'amount' you will be able to see, at a glance, how much money you have received for the month and how much money you have spent.

If you choose to set up your own accounts system, it is important that you are accurate and that you are aware of the items which the Inland Revenue will allow you to set against your tax liability.

Diaries and what to include

Many childminders choose to furnish parents of young children with a 'diary'. Although at first this may seem like even more paperwork, diaries can prove invaluable to both parents and practitioners. Diaries can be used to record a baby or young child's basic daily routine, and the diary goes back and forth between the child's home and the childminding setting. Both parents and childminders can also use the book to record additional information, such as what the baby has been like over the weekend, any new developments, any medicinal arrangements, holiday dates, etc. Although the diary should not take the place of face-to-face conversation, it can prove effective for parents who are often in a rush in a morning and worry that they may forget to say something important.

A typical page from a diary written for a 15-month-old child may read something like this:

DIARY EXTRACT

Monday 2nd July 2013

Breakfast – Lucinda ate half a bowl of porridge with sliced banana and drank all her milk.

Lunch – Lucinda ate all her lunch today. She had cottage pie, carrots and cauliflower followed by yoghurt.

Tea – Lucinda ate very little at teatime. She had ¼ of a cheese sandwich, some melon slices and a fromage frais.

From this diary entry Lucinda's parents are able to see at a glance what their daughter has eaten throughout the day. If she appears hungry towards the end of the day, they will be able to see that this is probably because Lucinda ate little at teatime at the childminders.

The childminder should also record the child's nappy changes or potty/ toilet routines. A child who has not had a bowel movement for a couple of days may be in some discomfort. Often this sort of thing can get overlooked as the parent may think that the child has gone to the toilet in the child-minding setting and the childminder will think that the child has had a bowel movement at home. By recording this information it is easy to see at a glance whether there is any cause for concern.

Likewise, a tired child can easily be identified if the childminder records sleep patterns or if the parent uses the diary to inform the childminder if they have had a bad night with the child waking often.

A brief description of the child's overall day, like the example on the following page, stating what they have enjoyed in the setting is often appreciated by parents who then feel they have had an insight into what their child is doing in their absence. It makes good sense to involve parents as much as possible in the care of their child even if they cannot be with them.

DIARY EXTRACT

Lucinda has enjoyed her day in the setting. She has enjoyed finger-painting using a variety of colours and has also produced some beautiful pictures using sponges and rollers. She has also enjoyed taking part in outdoor play using the ride-on toys and playing in the sand and water tray. She has managed to complete several jigsaws with some support, listened to stories and enjoyed singing songs and dressing up.

Development files

Childminders should produce a development file on each of the children in their care showing how the seven areas of learning are accessed. The file should demonstrate, through both short and more detailed observations (see Chapter Three), the child's current progress and show what measures are in place to guide the child towards future learning and development. The example below shows how a short observation can be recorded to go in a child's development file.

The two next examples are of longer observations. These more detailed observations should be carried out at least once a month and should contain more information regarding what the child is currently confident at and how you, the practitioner, can steer them towards their next goals. Photographs can also be included with these observations.

DETAILED OBSERVATION 1

Child's Name **Joe Bloggs**	
M/F **Male**	Date of Birth **17/01/10**
Date of Observation **11/07/13**	Time of Observation **10.30am**
Observer **Childminder**	

Observation – What is happening? What is being said?
Joe is playing in the sandpit with the cars and trucks. He picks up an aeroplane. 'Look aeroplane,' he says. I reply by asking him what colour it is.
   'Yellow,' he answers correctly. He then places the aeroplane back in the sand and looks up at me, smiling.
   'What else can you find? What about a blue one?' I ask. Joe quickly picks up a blue truck. Joe and I continue to do this for a short time. Joe correctly identifies the colours green, red and orange. After he had identified all the colours, Joe gave himself a big clap!

What does this tell me about the child's learning and development? How involved was the child?
Joe is getting confident at naming and identifying colours. He shows interest in this activity and is actively involved.

How can we sustain and extend the child's interest?
I can sustain and extend Joe's interests by introducing opportunities to match different colours, for example two red objects.

Personal, Social and Emotional Development

Communication and Language

Physical Development

Literacy

Mathematics

Understanding the World **Joe is exploring and investigating in the sand.**

Expressive Arts and Design **Joe is exploring media and materials.**

DETAILED OBSERVATION 2

Child's Name **Joe Bloggs**

M/F **Male** Date of Birth **17/01/10**

Date of Observation **22/08/13** Time of Observation **2.30pm**

Observer **Childminder**

Observation – What is happening? What is being said?
Joe is playing with the large bricks on the floor with his friend. His friend, who is a year older than Joe, suggests that they build a tower. 'Yeah,' Joe replies excitedly. He then begins placing bricks on top of each other. He lines the bricks up straight with the bottom brick and then fits them together so they join correctly. He continues to fit the bricks together until he has made a tower that is as tall as him.
   'Look,' he says to me when he has finished.
   'Shall we count your bricks, Joe?' I ask. Joe begins to count, pointing to the bottom brick first. He then proceeds up the tower counting seven bricks with confidence. When he has finished he sits back and looks at his friend who puts three bricks together.
   'Three bricks there,' Joe says, pointing to the bricks.

What does this tell me about the child's learning and development? How involved was the child?
Joe can confidently count up to seven independently. He can recognise the quantity of a group of objects.

How can we sustain and extend the child's interest?
To continue to develop Joe's counting skills. To provide opportunities to look at quantities, e.g. groups of two, three, four, five, etc.

Personal, Social and Emotional Development

Communication and Language

Physical Development

Literacy

Mathematics **Numbers and labels for counting.**

Understanding the World

Expressive Arts and Design **Joe is designing and making.**

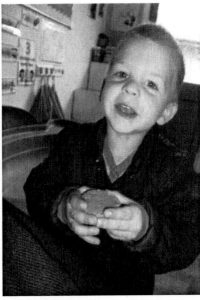

Reece enjoys modelling playdough. He is confident making shapes and recognises the different colours.

Writing policies

As a self-employed person running your own business from home it is important to always remember that, although you are providing a service, your house is still your home and as such should be treated with respect.

You will need to decide, prior to any child entering your setting, what your boundaries are going to be and how you are going to implement them. It is a good idea to think carefully about your aims and goals and write your policies to reflect these. Any policy you draw up should be displayed on the walls of your setting and a copy of each policy should be given to the parents of the child before a placement commences. Some childminders ask parents to sign a form to say that they understand and agree to their policies to avoid any future misunderstandings, but this is simply a matter of preference.

The main areas for which you may like to implement a policy are:

- **Behaviour**– Most parents accept the need for children to have boundaries when it comes to behaviour; however, it is important to realise that not all parents will share your views when it comes to discipline. You can usually determine early on whether or not a set of parents share your own views and values and this is one of the reasons why it is important to discuss things such as behaviour at the initial interview. You should be able to tell at this stage whether or not you feel able to work with the parents or whether you feel there would be too many conflicting opinions for you to offer suitable childcare. This is why I would never advise you to sign a contract on the first meeting – always try to allow yourself time to think and reflect on the interview and mull over the points and issues raised. When the time comes for the signing of contracts I would advise you to, once again, go over any policies you have and allow parents to ask any questions.

- **Confidentiality** – It is very important that you respect confidentiality at all times. You may be caring for children whose respective parents are friends or, worse still, enemies and they may at times try to glean information from you about the other families' circumstances. You must *never* partake in gossip or divulge any information about other families of the children you care for.

- **Equal Opportunities** – You must be aware of how you can promote equal opportunities by treating all the children, their parents and families as individuals and with equal concern. You must respect each family, their culture, belief, practice and religion and you must know how to discourage prejudice and stereotypical attitudes within your setting. It is important that you are confident at tackling discrimination and prejudicial remarks.

On the pages that follow are examples of the policies you could use. These policies can be adapted to suit your own requirements. On the next page is an example of a behaviour policy.

BEHAVIOUR POLICY

To enable all children to enjoy their time with me I have a few requests that
I would appreciate your help in achieving.

PLEASE be kind to others and polite at all times

PLEASE do not jump on the furniture

PLEASE do not run indoors

PLEASE be kind and gentle and treat others as you would like to be treated

PLEASE try to share and take turns

PLEASE take muddy shoes off at the door

PLEASE be honest and tell the truth

PLEASE REMEMBER we are all different, we have different ideas and
ways of doing things and that is what makes us all special

The things that you put in your own behaviour policy should reflect the
views you have on what is or is not acceptable to *you* in *your* own home. It is
a good idea to talk through the way you expect the children to behave, while
they are in your care, with the parents. They may have completely different
ideas of what constitutes acceptable behaviour and this is something that
must be cleared up early on. The children may be allowed to roam their own
home in muddy shoes and eat their lunch in front of the television but, if
this is something that you object to, you must make your own 'rules' clear
and ask that parents help you to implement them when they are bringing and
collecting their children.

The times when parents are in your home with their child are often the
times when things start to become unravelled. Children learn, from very early
on, what they can and cannot get away with and which adult is the 'soft touch'.
Often parents who are collecting their children after a long day at work indulge
their children out of tiredness or feelings of guilt but, if their children are using
your sofa as a trampoline, just because their parent is present and they know
this is something you have asked them not to do, then don't be afraid of telling
them to get down. *Never* allow the children to do something when their parent
is present that you would not allow them to do if they were not. It is confusing
to the children and undermines your authority in your own home.

It is often difficult to know what to say to someone who is asking you
questions about a child you care for. Although you do not wish to be rude
neither must you breach your confidentiality policy. Politely tell the person

that you are not at liberty to divulge information about the children or the families that you care for. An example of a confidentiality policy may look something like this:

CONFIDENTIALITY POLICY

You will appreciate that, as a childminder, I acquire some sensitive and private information and knowledge about the children that I care for, and their families.

As a professional practitioner I treat confidentiality very seriously and you can rest assured that the information you share with me will not be passed on to anyone else (except in very extreme circumstances when it may be in the interest of the child to do so).

Please help me to maintain confidentiality by refraining from asking me for any information relating to another child in my care.

Please remember that EVERYONE has the right to confidentiality and your help in maintaining this within my setting is much appreciated.

EQUAL OPPORTUNITIES POLICY

Regardless of their racial origins, cultural background, gender, age, family grouping or disability ALL children in my care will be:

Treated as individuals and with equal concern

Treated fairly and equally

Given the opportunity to develop and learn

Encouraged to learn about people different from themselves and to respect and enjoy those differences.

I intend to promote, at all times:

Respect of others, their culture, belief, practice and religion.

I intend to discourage at all times:

Stereotypical attitudes

Prejudice of any nature

Negative images.

I will not tolerate, at any time:

Discrimination towards any child because of their skin colour, gender, cultural or family background, racial origins or disability.

It is important, while ensuring that parents are aware of what you will and will not tolerate from children while they are on your premises, that you also make sure your expectations are realistic and that your methods for achieving your aims and goals are effective and take into account each child's age and understanding. You must realise that no two families are alike and therefore not everyone will be in complete agreement with you. There are many different forms of parenting and no one can reasonably say that their methods are right whilst others are wrong. As a childminder you must learn to understand, accept and tolerate a wide range of parenting ideas. If a parent does not agree with the boundaries and policies you have set, it is important to discuss any concerns they may have prior to signing the contract and try to compromise whenever possible.

If you feel it is necessary to revise or update your policies once you have been childminding for some time, then you must draw up a new policy, furnish the parents of the children with a copy and discuss any changes with them to ensure that everyone is aware of the changes and why you feel it is necessary to make them.

In addition to the above policies you should also set out an emergency plan showing details of the procedure you will follow in the event of an emergency and give a copy of this plan to the parents of the children in your care.

It is important that you obtain *written* parental permission for various procedures you may like to carry out within your setting. These procedures could be:

- taking a child on an outing
- taking photographs of the children in your care
- videoing an event the children are taking part in, such as a concert or birthday party
- transporting a child in a car
- seeking medical advice when necessary.

Suitable forms seeking permission for the above can be obtained from PACEY or you could devise your own forms and get the parents to sign them.

Safety checks

It is important, while going about your daily childminding duties, to be aware of how to continually check the toys and equipment you are using. Toys and equipment which are in constant use by several children will become broken and worn from time to time.

You should get into the habit of checking your toys daily, either when you get them out for the children to play with or at the end of the day when the children have gone home and you are tidying things away. I would recommend that toys are sorted and stored in suitable boxes so that you can see at a glance which toys are kept where. This is a good way of ensuring that the correct toys are given to the correct children. For example, a box which contains suitable toys for babies, such as rattles, soft toys etc., should not contain anything with small parts which could pose a threat to the children's safety. By storing your construction toys together, your puzzles and games together and your dressing-up and role-play items together, you can immediately find the correct toys to suit the needs of the children you are caring for and this prevents you from having to rummage through endless boxes, removing unsuitable items.

In addition to checking toys, you should set aside some time, say once a month, when you can spend some quality time carefully checking each item of equipment for wear and tear. You should make a note in your diary when the time is approaching for an equipment check and then devise a plan similar to the example below to record your findings. As well as the equipment you use indoors, you should also check your pushchairs and outdoor apparatus, such as swings, slides etc., and most importantly these items of play equipment should be checked after the winter months, when they have perhaps been used very little and adverse weather conditions could have affected their safety and suitability.

Risk assessments are vital in the childminding setting and these assessments must identify which aspects of the environment and equipment need to be checked on a regular basis, and you need to keep a record of what has been checked, when it was checked and by whom.

It is the responsibility of you, the childminder, to ensure that all reasonable steps have been taken to ensure the safety of the children and reduce any hazards to the children on the premises both indoors and outdoors.

The EYFS statutory guidance gives three points of consideration for childcare practitioners to consider with regard to risk assessment and these are as follows.

- The risk assessment should cover anything with which a child may come into contact.

- The premises and equipment should be clean, and providers should be aware of the requirements of health and safety legislation (including hygiene requirements). This should include informing and keeping staff up to date.

- A health and safety policy should be in place, which includes procedures of identifying, reporting and dealing with accidents, hazards and faulty equipment.

EQUIPMENT CHECK CHART

DATE OF CHECK	ITEM	FINDINGS	REPAIRED/ REPLACED	CHECKED BY
17th May	Constructions toys	2 toys with broken parts	1 replaced, 1 mended	Karen
19th May	Highchair	Frayed reins	Replaced reins	Karen
22nd May	Potty	Split in plastic	Replaced	Karen
22nd May	Outdoor climbing frame	Screw loose by ladder	Repaired	Karen

Fire drills

It is important to carry out regular fire drills while going about your child-minding duties. Fire drills should be practised with the children so that they are aware of what is expected of them in the case of a fire. Children who are old enough should be taught an effective method of evacuating the house and they should realise the importance of remaining calm and doing exactly as they are told. It is a good idea to make a chart for your fire drills similar to the one in the example below and make a note in your diary, say once every couple of months, to practise the drill. You should change the days and times that you practise the drill frequently in order that *all* the children get the chance to take part. It is pointless doing your fire drill every Monday if you have several children who only attend your setting on Thursday and Friday.

FIRE DRILL CHART

DATE	TIME	NUMBER OF CHILDREN	EFFECTIVENESS OF DRILL/ IMPROVEMENTS NECESSARY	NEXT DRILL
Mon 02/07/13	11.15am	1 – age 3 1 – age 6 months	Very effective – older child understood and carried out requests calmly.	
Fri 06/07/13	2.30 pm	2 – age 2	Took a little longer than I would have liked to get the children out of the building. Decided to practice the drill again next week with these particular children.	

Chapter 6
Outstanding... Early Identification and Intervention

Working in partnership with other organisations is absolutely vital in order to identify any additional needs and to safeguard the children in your care. As a childminder it can often be quite daunting when you think something is amiss, and these feelings are heightened when you have no one to talk to with regard to your suspicions.

Not wanting to upset parents or being frightened of 'getting it wrong' are not, however, adequate reasons for ignoring any warning signs and it is important to remember that you must act on any concerns you may have as it is your responsibility to ensure that you have the child's best interests at heart at all times, even if this may initially make things difficult for you.

Early identification

Identifying a problem may be relatively easy if you are caring for a child regularly and, depending on the nature of your relationship with the child's parents – hopefully because you have read and understood the importance of relationships in Chapter Two – you will be able to discuss your concerns with the parents. For example, you may notice that a child you are caring for is having difficulty following simple instructions. This may be simply because they don't want to or it could be down to underlying hearing problems. A quick chat with the parents may reveal that the child has had a cold or an ear infection that you had been unaware of, or it may reveal other issues which may need addressing with the help of the child's general practitioner. Either way, when you have identified a problem, no matter how small – and let's face it, the smaller the concern the easier it is to sort out – you MUST do something about it. Identifying a problem and ignoring it is worse than not having noticed it in the first place.

Early intervention

When you have identified a concern with regard to a child's development, it is vital that you speak to the parents initially. If, after having spoken to them, you are still concerned and the parents share your concerns, then it is time to work together in partnership with other professionals in order to decide on the best outcome for the child. Working with other agencies in this way is known as 'Early Intervention' and may include working with inclusion officers, special educational needs coordinators (SENCO), speech therapists or social workers.

If a child in your care is showing signs of requiring support from an outside agency, it is crucial that you get the agreement of the parents. Without parental consent there is very little that you can do except to support the child to the best of your ability and continually share your concerns with the parents. Parents need to know that their child is not being 'labelled' and that the intervention is to ensure that the child's best interests are supported. It is important to stress that outside agencies are responsible for working *with* parents rather than *for* them and that the support they can provide is far-reaching and of great benefit to the child.

Although you may be helping to identify a potential problem, it is essential that you focus on the positive things, in order to help the parents to cope with the fact that their child may require support from outside agencies. Painting a picture of complete doom and gloom can frighten off parents and may even push them into refusing any necessary help and this, in turn, will have an adverse affect on the child. Telling the parent of a child who appears to have slight hearing problems that you think their child may be 'deaf' is, for example, extreme. Always remember that you are the childminder; you are not an expert on hearing problems and you cannot and must not attempt to diagnose a child. Even if prompted by the parent, always refrain from giving your own 'opinion'. State the facts, backed up with observations, and make sure that you are there to support the child and the parents in whatever they decide to do.

If the parents are in agreement, it may be necessary to request the help of an inclusion officer and you will need to complete the necessary referral form. Here is an example of a referral form.

CONFIDENTIAL INFORMATION
REFERRAL FORM: CHILDCARE INCLUSION TEAM

Referred by:	Agency:	Date:
Name of Child:	D.O.B	Age:
Parent/Carer:	Gender:	Ethnicity:
Family Address:	Setting Name & Address:	
	SENCO:	
	Key person:	
Tel Number:	Email:	

Child looked after by the local authority (LAC)

Stage on SEN Code Practice:

- Setting expressing concern

- Early Years Action

- EYA Plus

- Statutory Assessment In Progress

- Statement

Has there been a Common Assessment (CAF) completed?

About the child: (brief account of strengths, areas of interest and needs)

Reason for referral: (brief account of reason for support)

What strategies have you worked with so far?

Evidence: (required to support the referral; for example, observations, reports, minutes, etc.)

Other agencies involved:

- Health visitor

- Paediatrician

- Speech therapist

- Home portage

- Sensory service

- Child development centre

- Autism outreach

- Educational psychologist

- Other (please specify)

Describe the contact you have had with other agencies and the method; for example, telephone, visits, meetings etc.

Record of the child's attendance in setting: days and times

Monday	AM	PM
Tuesday	AM	PM
Wednesday	AM	PM
Thursday	AM	PM
Friday	AM	PM

Parent/carer signature ....

On behalf of the setting ....

Child abuse and safeguarding

In addition to identifying any learning or development issues that a child may have, it is also the responsibility of the childminder to ensure that they are fully aware of all safeguarding issues and that they are confident in spotting any signs of child abuse.

Identifying and acting on suspicions of child abuse can be very traumatic and many practitioners, even those with years of experience, will still shy away from reporting suspicions of this nature. An outstanding childminder, however, is well trained and knowledgeable on all aspects of child abuse and safeguarding and they will be confident in knowing what to do should they find themselves in the position of caring for a child who has been, or who appears to be, suffering from abuse.

Child abuse is behaviour that causes significant harm to a child. There are four types of child abuse and these are defined below:

- **Emotional abuse** – This is when a child is deprived of love and affection. They may be repeatedly rejected or humiliated.

- **Sexual abuse** – This is when a child is directly or indirectly exploited or corrupted by involving them in inappropriate sexual activities. Showing children pornographic material is also classed as sexual abuse.

- **Physical abuse** – This is when a child is hurt physically, including hitting, kicking or inflicting pain. Poisoning, drowning or smothering are also forms of physical abuse.

- **Neglect** – This is when a child is denied appropriate care, including love, attention, safety, nourishment, warmth, education and medical attention.

Abuse can have long-lasting traumatic effects which can damage a child's development emotionally, physically and psychologically. A child who has been abused may grow up with feelings of inadequacy and have difficulty forming happy relationships. Some may even become abusers themselves.

Children have the need and right to be in an environment where they feel happy, safe and secure and it is your duty, as a childminder, to ensure that these needs are met and, should you suspect that a child in your care is being abused, you must act upon your suspicions. It is not an option to ignore or turn a blind eye to your suspicions hoping that someone else will deal with the problem. You have a duty and responsibility to put the child's needs and welfare first.

In order to try to understand abuse and why it occurs, you must first be aware that it can occur in any family structure. Abuse does not discriminate and it is important that you do not assume that it can only happen to children from poor families or single-parent families. Even children from 'respectable' backgrounds can be subjected to abuse.

In most cases children who suffer from abuse do so at the hands of someone who is known to them. Although it has been suggested that a high proportion of abusers have themselves been abused and, therefore, know of no other way of dealing with children, this is not always the case. Abuse is often the result of a combination of social, economic, medical, environmental and psychological reasons and it is important to remember that children of any age can be vulnerable to abuse.

Types of abuse

- **Emotional abuse** – A child who is constantly deprived of love and affection will quickly lose confidence and become nervous and withdrawn. Being subjected to continual threatening behaviour in

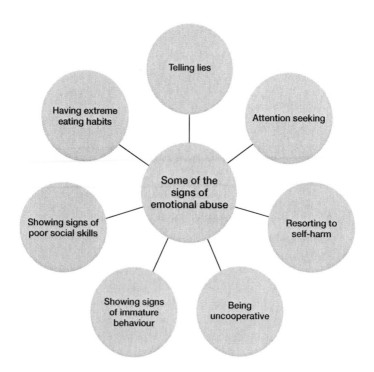

the form of verbal abuse or shouting can have lasting effects on a child. It is very difficult to see any signs of emotional abuse as the effects are rarely physical. Children who are subjected to emotional abuse are often vulnerable and have a low opinion of themselves. They constantly crave attention and will often put their trust into anyone who shows them any sign of affection.

- **Sexual abuse** – A child who is used by an adult for their own gratification is said to be sexually abused. It is very important to remember that not all sexual abusers are male. Children may be subjected to sexual abuse through bribery, threats or physical force and sexual abuse can take the form of fondling, masturbation, sexual intercourse, oral sex, exhibitionism or through the showing of pornographic materials. A child who is being sexually abused may show both physical and emotional signs.

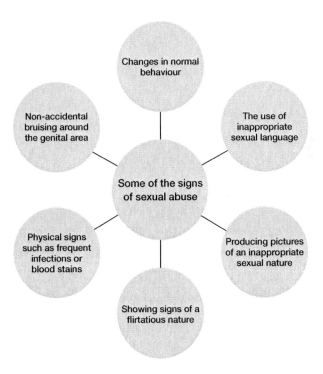

- **Physical abuse** – A child exposed to physical abuse is suffering
  from the deliberate infliction of pain and injury. Physical abuse
  may take many forms and includes hitting, shaking, biting, burning,
  cutting, squeezing and poisoning.

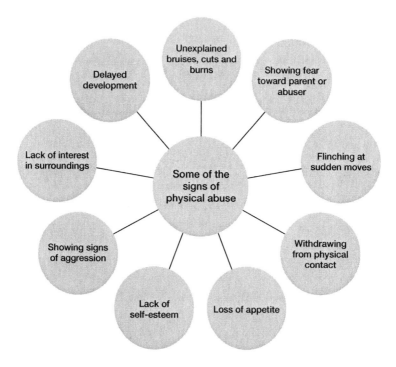

- **Neglect** – A parent who persistently fails to provide the basic
  physical needs for their child is guilty of neglect. Neglect can take
  many forms, including failing to provide adequate food or clothing,
  failing to seek medical advice when necessary, or leaving the child
  unattended.

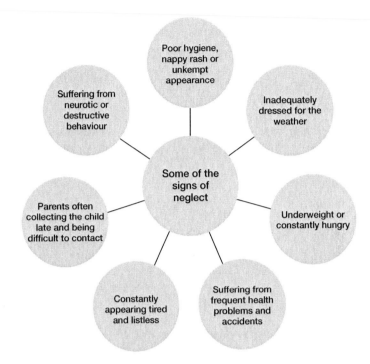

It is important to remember that no two children are the same and no two circumstances will mirror one another. It is for this reason that you must remember that those shown in the examples are the most *common* signs of abuse and a child may suffer from one or more of the symptoms. As a childminder you will be in the best possible situation to monitor a child's behaviour and will inevitably notice any changes almost immediately. Unlike children who attend nursery schools and may be cared for by several different carers, you will have built up a trusting relationship with the child and should notice any worrying signs, symptoms or changes in their usual behaviour.

Common sites for accidental and non-accidental injuries

The lists below show the *common* sites for both accidental and non-accidental injuries.

Common sites for *accidental* injuries are:

- forehead
- chin
- nose
- knees
- elbows

- forearms
- spine
- hip
- shins.

Common sites for *non-accidental* injuries are:

- lips and mouth
- eyes
- ears
- cheeks
- skull
- chest
- stomach

- buttocks
- back
- back of legs
- upper and inner arms
- genital or rectal areas
- soles of the feet.

Although the above sites are the most common sites for injuries, you must bear in mind that not all injuries on the shins, for example, may be accidental. Persistent or experienced abusers will often try to hide the injuries they inflict on the child or make them *appear* accidental. It is just as important to recognise the *type* of injury as well as the *site* of the injury when trying to decide whether any abuse has taken place.

Different types of injuries you might encounter

- **Bruising** – When the result of an accident, bruises are usually scattered and irregular. Bruises which are the same colour suggest they occurred at around the same time. It is important not to confuse birthmarks or Mongolian blue spots with bruises. When bruising is non-accidental it may appear in the shape of an implement which has been used to inflict the injury, such as a belt or buckle. The bruises will be regular and of varying colours, indicating both old and new bruises. Bruising on the lips, eyes, ears and mouth are usually associated with non-accidental injuries.

- **Burns and scalds** – The parent of a child who has suffered from an accidental burn or scald should furnish you with details of the injury and offer a logical explanation. Medical attention should have been sought in severe circumstances and the wound should be dressed appropriately. When a burn or scald is not accidental, it may appear in difficult-to-reach places, such as the buttocks or back, and therefore would not suggest self-infliction. The burn may take on the appearance of the object which was used to inflict the injury, such as a cigarette.

  - **Fractures and breaks** – Broken bones in young children are most common on the arms and legs and, occasionally, the ribs. Children under the age of two years rarely experience accidental fractures. Broken bones or fractures in varying stages of healing should be viewed as suspicious.

  - **Genital Injuries** – Many young children suffer from constipation or threadworms and discomfort around the anus may be suffered as a result of this. Nappy rash in babies may also cause soreness and blistering. However, you should treat any bruising, bleeding or infection of the genital areas with suspicion.

  - **Cuts and grazes** – Accidental cuts and grazes are usually minor and require no treatment. Deep incisions or large untreated scratches should be viewed with suspicion.

  - **Bites** – A child may sometimes be bitten by another child in the course of everyday play. However, bite marks which are too large to be inflicted by another child or those which show an adult teeth pattern should give cause for concern.

There are many factors which may be associated with child abuse and it is important that you do not make any assumptions as to the kind of people who are likely to inflict abuse on their children. As I have mentioned before, there is no set pattern for abuse and it can occur in any family structure. As a childminder you must be vigilant when assessing the evidence you have and avoid stereotyping gender, as this may result in signs of abuse being ignored. For example, a boy who shows a lack of emotion and appears dirty and unkempt may be seen by some as a typical boy who prefers to be independent and enjoys getting dirty. However, it may also mean that signs of neglect are being unrecognised. Would the same assumptions apply if it was a girl who was dirty, unkempt and lacking in emotion?

Disclosures of abuse

In addition to you actually noticing possible signs or symptoms of child abuse which give you cause for concern, it may be that a child themselves provides you with a disclosure of abuse.

There are two ways in which a child may disclose the possibility that they are being abused:

Overt disclosure – This is when a child actually approaches you and tells you verbally what is happening to them.

Covert disclosure – This is when a child uses pictures, play or body language to draw your attention to what may be happening to them. Covert disclosures are less obvious and should be interpreted carefully keeping things in proportion without ignoring the evidence.

If you suspect a child is being abused, it is essential that you act upon your suspicions. Listen to what the child tells you, without interrupting, asking questions or prompting them. Stay calm and talk to the child in a manner appropriate to their level of understanding.

If a child tells you they have been abused:

- Stay calm.
- Speak to the child gently and allow them plenty of time to tell you in *their own words* what they want to say.
- Never ask leading questions or point the finger of blame.
- Do not interrupt the child or put words into their mouth if they are having difficulty expressing their feelings.
- Offer reassurance and tell the child they have done the right thing by confiding in you.
- Never promise to keep their disclosure a secret. You will not be able to keep this promise and you could seriously harm a child who has placed their trust in you and then feels you have let them down.

Recording signs of abuse

Any child in your care who has suffered from an injury, however minor, should have this injury recorded. If a child arrives at your home with an injury, you should seek an explanation from the parent about the nature of the injury and record the details. These records would be absolutely vital in a child-abuse case. A child may be suffering from injuries or neglect over a sustained period of time and it is only by carefully logging injuries and incidents that you and other professionals may be able to recognise a pattern of abuse forming. The records you keep, while primarily for the protection of the child, should be kept with the cooperation of the parents.

When recording details of injuries or suspicions it is vital that you stick to the *facts*. Never let your own opinions or judgements hamper your reasoning and, if a child discloses an incident of abuse, record what they have said *exactly* using their own words and do not be tempted to elaborate on or add to their disclosure.

Procedures to follow if you suspect child abuse

All child carers have a duty to report their suspicions relating to abuse. It is perfectly normal that you should feel apprehensive and scared. You may feel that you are betraying the child's parents or that you have jumped to conclusions. However, if you are familiar with the signs and symptoms of neglect, and you have any reasonable doubts about the safety of a child in your care, you have a duty to report your suspicions. It is the welfare of the child which must take priority at all times.

If it is appropriate, you may like to speak to the child's parents first about the change in their child's behaviour or if the child has said something to you which is giving you cause for concern. The nature of your suspicions and the relationship you have with the parents may, however, make speaking to them difficult or inappropriate. It is vital that you are open and honest with the person (and/or their family where appropriate) from the outset about why, what, how and with whom information will, or could be shared, and seek their agreement, unless it is unsafe or inappropriate to do so.

All childminders should be aware of the procedure which they are expected to follow, should they suspect a child in their care is being abused or neglected, and you should ensure that you are familiar with this procedure; each local authority will have their own procedure to follow, so ensure you are aware of what it is. You may report your concerns to the appropriate authority or, alternatively, you may prefer to contact the NSPCC. Both social services and the NSPCC have a duty to investigate any reports they receive. It is vital that you remain professional at all times, only report the *facts* and respect confidentiality.

After you have reported your concerns to the appropriate authority, a decision will be made by them as to whether a referral should be made. This is where the information supplied by you may be crucial in building up a background of knowledge about the child. It may be that no action is taken at this stage and you may be requested to continue to monitor the situation and record any further concerns you may have. If, however, it is decided that further action needs to be taken, this will be done by social services and not by *you*. Although you should be informed that a response has been made, you will not be notified of the action taken as this will remain confidential with the child protection agencies. If action is taken it will be necessary to interview the child and contact the parents. Enquiries may be made from other professionals, such as doctors, health visitors, schools, etc., to build up an accurate picture of the child's situation. In some cases a child protection conference may be arranged. However, it is not always necessary for the childminder to attend.

Allegations against childminders

There may be times when an allegation is made against you. At times like these it is important to record everything that has been said and, if you are a member of PACEY, it is a good idea for you to contact them and seek their advice. You may experience a variety of feelings including anger, upset and distress if an allegation is made against you. However, it is important that you remain calm and deal with any allegations rationally. Listen to what the parent has to say and then calmly put your own point of view across and explain the situation in your own words. Childminders and nannies are particularly vulnerable to allegations as they usually work alone and do not have the added support of co-workers. The teenage sons of childminders are particularly vulnerable to having accusations made against them and you should consider protecting yourself and your family in the following ways:

- Behave in a professional manner at all times.
- Maintain confidentiality at all times.
- Report any concerns or suspicions you may have about ill-treatment or abuse to the appropriate authorities.
- Keep accurate up-to-date records of any accidents or injuries to children in your care.
- Ensure that you tell parents of any accidents or injuries to their child immediately.
- Ensure that you notify parents immediately if you notice a change in their child's usual behaviour.
- Never handle a child roughly or inflict physical punishment.
- Never ask a child for a cuddle; always take your cue from them.
- Never allow children to be cared for by someone who is not authorised to do so.
- Always act in a responsible manner while in the company of children and use appropriate language.
- Never leave the children unattended.
- Encourage children to become independent as soon as possible, particularly when carrying out personal tasks such as visiting the toilet.
- Keep up to date with your own training.
- Teach children how to protect themselves and stay safe.

Where to seek support

If you have had to deal with an incident of child abuse or have had an allegation made against you or a member of your family, you will probably be experiencing a wide range of feelings. It is vital that you seek support to deal with your own feelings and you may like to do this by contacting:

- PACEY, if you are a member
- social workers
- your health visitor
- your doctor
- a child protection officer.

Chapter 7
Outstanding... Progress Reports

The revised Early Years Foundation Stage states that all practitioners must carry out a progress check on the children in their care at the age of two years. Previously progress checks were carried out before children left the setting to start formal schooling; however, it has now been recognised that, by assessing a child's development at two years, it is possible to discover any significant emerging concerns or identify any special educational needs or disabilities.

Progress checks for two-year-olds

The two year progress check should take into account the prime areas of development which are personal, social and emotional development, communication and language and physical development. However, beyond these areas it is the responsibility of the practitioner to decide what the summary should include, though it does need to take into account:

- the areas where the children are progressing well
- the areas where the children may require any additional support
- the areas where any developmental delay has been recognised
- the areas where any concerns have been highlighted.

It is very important that the summary of development is shared with parents and an effective plan should be developed, whereby parents and practitioners can work together to ensure that children are being supported equally in both the home environment and the setting.

The example below shows an Early Years Foundation Stage progress report.

EARLY YEARS FOUNDATION STAGE PROGRESS REPORT

Name of child:	Date of birth:
Length of time in setting:	Date of completion of report:
Childminder's name:	
Personal, social and emotional development:	
Communication and language:	
Physical development:	
Mathematics:	
Literacy:	
Understanding the world:	
Expressive arts and design:	
Comments – parents:	
Comments – child:	
Next steps:	

The progress report must contain comments about the characteristics of effective learning, which are evident throughout all areas of learning, and these are:

- playing and exploring
- active learning
- creating and thinking critically.

The above three characteristics underpin learning and development across *all* areas and support the children.

The main aims

The main aims of the two year progress check are to:

- provide the parents with a clear and accurate account of their children's development
- ensure that practitioners understand the needs of the children and how to plan future activities in order to meet these needs effectively
- ensure that parents understand the needs of their children and how, with the support of the practitioner, they can meet these needs effectively at home
- ensure that a clear plan of action is evident to address any development concerns where necessary – this may include working with other professionals.

Including the children in progress checks

It is very important that progress checks are carried out by a practitioner who knows the children well and, for you, as the childminder, this should be relatively easy as you will quite probably be solely responsible for the care of the children unless you work with an assistant. You will need to use your everyday observations of the children as discussed in Chapter Three to successfully complete the progress check and you should be including the views and contributions of the children's parents. It is also a necessary requirement that children are able to actively contribute to the check and you should, therefore, be involving the children in the whole process, asking them appropriate questions and taking into account their views and ideas. This may be easier to do with some children than with others, depending on their development.

Using observations in progress checks

It is essential that you recognise the links between ongoing observations of children and the two year progress check and that you understand how these fit together in the assessment cycle:

Observations:
Children's interests and achievements are considered.
Parental contributions are explored.
Children's contributions are included.

Identifying children learning priorities:
Childminder and parents work together to support the children's learning in the setting and at home with the use of the observations described above.

Planning:
Childminders plan appropriately to support the learning and development of the children.

Completing the progress check

When completing the progress check you may find it helpful to prepare a draft, outlining some initial judgements that you have made from the evidence you have, based on your observations of the children. It will be necessary for you to:

- discuss your findings with the children's parents
- invite parental contributions.

It is important to remember that parents must be involved in the whole process of the progress check and that the information you supply is:

- clear and easy to understand
- free of jargon and terminology which may not be familiar to the parents

- accurate and up to date, showing a true picture of the children's current stage of progress and development

- able to define the areas where the children's progress is slower than expected.

By law children only need a progress check at the age of two. If a child is leaving the setting to go to school they will have the two year progress check (assuming the child was in the setting at this age) along with a 'transition form'. If the child leaves the setting before the age of two for any reason then they will have the observations only.

Chapter 8
Outstanding... Foundations

In this chapter we will look in depth at how childminders can set the foundations to ensure that the children in their setting achieve the five outcomes set out by the Government. These outcomes are:

- be healthy

- stay safe

- enjoy and achieve

- make a positive contribution

- achieve economic well-being.

How can childminders help children to be healthy?

The aims of this outcome are:

- to ensure that children and young people are physically healthy

- to ensure that children and young people are mentally and emotionally healthy

- to ensure that children and young people live healthy lifestyles.

Encouraging children to lead a healthy lifestyle is very important. By instilling the importance of being healthy from a young age, it is possible to help to combat obesity and encourage children to take responsibility for their own healthy lifestyle. Learning about healthy eating and exercise early on in life should help children to make the right choices and understand why these choices are necessary for their long-term health.

Children are naturally interested in their own bodies. They are curious about how their bodies work, how the heart beats, what the lungs are for and how their muscles work. By encouraging children to develop this interest and curiosity, it will be easier to explain to them why a healthy lifestyle, i.e. a balanced diet, fresh air and exercise, is important.

Firstly, children need to learn about healthy eating. Most children enjoy sweets, chocolate and fizzy drinks. However, we now know that these foods, though nice to eat, do not provide our bodies with any nutritional value and, therefore, it is important that sweets and fizzy drinks are kept to a minimum and are offered rarely, perhaps as a treat, rather than regularly or in place of meals.

Some children are 'fussy eaters' and will moan and complain if they are not given the snacks and sugary foods they desire. However, it is important that childminders realise that children will only 'crave' these foods for a short time until the body has been weaned off this need for sugar.

In order to provide children with a healthy diet, childminders need to understand what constitutes 'nutritional' food and how they can go about planning and preparing a menu which will both appeal to children and provide them with the necessary nutrients their body needs.

The main food groups

There are five main food groups. These are:

- bread, cereals and potatoes
- fruit and vegetables
- meat, fish and pulses
- milk and dairy products
- products containing fat and sugar.

Bread, cereals and potatoes – This category includes bread, pasta, oats, rice, noodles and breakfast cereals. Every meal offered to children should contain at least one of the food products from this group. Wholemeal bread and brown rice are preferable to white bread and white rice as they contain more vitamins.

Fruit and vegetables – This category includes all fruit and vegetables, except potatoes which are included in the above-mentioned food group. You (with the child's parents) should be aiming to provide children with at least five portions of fruit and vegetables per day. Foods from this category can be fresh, canned or frozen or served as juices. If choosing canned fruit, make sure that you purchase fruit in their natural juices rather than in syrup as the syrup contains a high level of sugar. Canned vegetables should be purchased in water rather than brine which contains a high level of salt.

Meat, fish and pulses – This category contains all types of meat products, such as burgers and sausages, poultry, fish and eggs. Vegetarians would include soya products and tofu in this category. Lentils and pulses are also included. You and the child's parents should be aiming to provide two portions of food from this category per day.

Milk and dairy products – This category includes milk, cheese and yoghurt. For a healthy balanced diet, children should be offered two or three servings from this category per day.

Products containing fat and sugar – This category includes butter, margarine, oil, biscuits, cakes, ice-cream, chips and other fried foods, sweets, jam and fizzy drinks. You should be aiming to serve only small quantities from this food group on an occasional basis.

The different types of nutrients

The five different types of nutrients which the body requires are:

- carbohydrates
- proteins
- fats
- vitamins
- minerals.

Carbohydrates – The main function of carbohydrates is to supply the body with energy. Carbohydrates can be broken down into two forms and these are 'simple' carbohydrates which can be turned into energy quickly and are found in fizzy drinks, sugar, biscuits, cakes, etc., and 'complex' carbohydrates which take longer to be turned into energy and can be found in pasta, bread, potatoes, breakfast cereals, etc. A lack of carbohydrates in the diet would result in tiredness and difficulty concentrating.

Proteins – The muscles, hair, nails, skin and internal organs of our bodies are made of protein. For our bodies to grow properly and repair themselves when necessary we need a good source of protein in our diets. Protein can be found in meat, poultry, fish, milk and milk products, eggs, beans and nuts.

Fats – Fat provides the body with energy. It also provides the body with insulation and protects our internal organs. Fats can be found in cheese, meat, butter, lard, chocolate, nuts, oily fish, etc.

Vitamins – Our bodies cannot make vitamins and, therefore, it is essential that we eat food products which contain them. A varied diet will ensure that we consume the correct amount of each of the vitamins as listed below:

- **Vitamin A** is found in liver, carrots and dark green vegetables such as cabbage. Vitamin A maintains good vision, skin and hair.

- **Vitamin B** is found in liver, cereals, beans and eggs and helps to break down the food we eat in order for it to give us energy. Vitamin B also helps the body to produce blood.

- **Vitamin C** is found in most fresh fruit and vegetables and, in particular, citrus fruits such as oranges and lemons. Vitamin C helps the body to fight infection and maintain healthy skin.

- **Vitamin D** is found in oily fish and eggs and helps to build strong teeth and bones.

- **Vitamin E** is found in whole grains, nuts and dark-green leafy vegetables such as cabbage. Vitamin E helps to protect our body cells from damage.

Minerals – Although our bodies need a huge range of minerals in order to remain healthy, the three main minerals required are iron, calcium and iodine.

Essential non-nutrient foods

In addition to the above food groups, bodies also need fibre and water. Fibre and water are essential for bodies to be able to grow and function correctly and these products are known as non-nutrient foods, because they do not provide us with any energy.

Preferences, eating habits, allergies and culture

In order to provide children with a healthy balanced diet, you, as the child-minder, also need to take into account their preferences, eating habits at home, allergies and culture.

- **Preferences** – As a childminder, you should be aiming to provide the children in your care with a healthy balanced diet. However, there is little point in preparing a healthy meal if you have used ingredients which the children do not like. The children's likes and dislikes should be taken into consideration when planning your menu.

- **Eating habits at home** – This can be very difficult. If children are used to eating 'chips with everything' at home, it may be difficult to get them to enjoy a healthy meal while in the childminding setting. You need to plan and prepare your meals with the parents of the children you are caring for, and any issues and eating habits should come to light when discussing your meals with them. Try to work out a suitable strategy which will encourage the children and parents to adopt a healthy attitude to food, both in the setting and at home. Always start by making small, manageable changes. For example, a child who has come to expect chips with every meal will find it completely unacceptable if you impose a total ban on chips. However, by reducing the amount of meals which include chips and substituting them with a healthy alternative, perhaps two or three times a week, you will set the wheels in motion for a healthier lifestyle, which you can then build on gradually.

- **Allergies** – Childhood allergies can be quite common and you need to be prepared to work with the parents and the children you are caring for to ensure that you do not offer any food products which may be harmful to the children. Diabetes, milk allergies, coeliac disease, etc., are all complaints that may affect children.

Food intolerances and allergies

Food intolerances and allergies occur when an individual has an unpleasant reaction to a specific food. Reactions may include:

- vomiting
- diarrhoea
- abdominal pain
- constipation
- bloated stomach
- skin rashes
- headaches.

Some of the foods which are most commonly associated with intolerance and allergies are:

- cow's milk
- shellfish
- nuts
- gluten.

Having the right approach to healthy eating

Although, as I have already said, ensuring children eat a healthy diet is a major part of your job as a childminder, it is important, while instilling the need for healthy eating, that you do not become 'obsessed' with food and allow this obsession to rub off on the children. This may lead to problems in later life, such as eating disorders like anorexia and bulimia. It is not necessary to ban all foods which are not considered healthy; it is simply a case of eating these food products in moderation and not substituting chocolate bars and puddings for a healthy balanced meal. Your aim is to try to get the children to understand what constitutes healthy food so that, in time, they will learn to choose these healthy options for themselves as a way of life, rather than because they feel they have to!

One of the easiest ways to start children on a healthy diet is to change the way you offer snacks. Many children would opt for a biscuit and fizzy drink; however, by offering a plate of brightly coloured fruits that look appealing and freshly prepared fruit juices along with carrot sticks and raisins, you will be giving the children plenty of choice from a range of healthy foods without curbing the appetite. Everyone eats unhealthy foods some of the time and you should not make children feel guilty for giving in to their cravings occasionally. It is when unhealthy foods are chosen on a regular basis that the risk of serious health problems are increased, and these may, sadly, last a lifetime.

Physical exercise

In addition to offering children a healthy balanced diet, it is also important that you include physical exercise in their daily routines. Physical exercise should not just be kept for outdoors, although playing outdoors is essential and should be incorporated in your everyday routines in order for the children to get the fresh air they need to remain healthy.

Indoor physical exercise may come in the form of:

- obstacle courses
- dance
- action rhymes
- playing games such as 'Simon says' and 'Musical chairs'
- visiting a soft play gym.

Outdoor physical exercise may come in the form of:

- using ride-on toys
- obstacle courses
- ball games
- skipping
- races
- visiting the park or playground.

Providing a healthy setting

In order for you to help the children be healthy, you need to consider the extent to which your setting encourages children to understand and adopt healthy habits and the extent to which children can make healthy choices about what they eat and drink. For example, you need to ensure that:

- You offer a choice of healthy meals and snacks.
- You offer healthy drinks.
- You talk to the children about the importance of making healthy choices.
- You discuss with the children the importance of regular exercise.
- You set a good example yourself for healthy living.

Good mental health

In addition to keeping their bodies physically healthy, it is also important for childminders to promote the good mental health of the children under their care. Children need to be encouraged to sustain healthy emotional attachments with people in safe, secure and trusting relationships. Children thrive when their emotional needs are met and childminders need to ensure that they nurture their children's emotional, mental, social and spiritual well-being.

This can be done by:

- showing a genuine interest in the child
- acknowledging the child's strengths and weaknesses
- allowing the child freedom to choose
- valuing and praising the child's achievements
- showing clear and consistent boundaries.

Ensuring the children in your care are healthy

You can ensure that the children in your care are healthy by:

- promoting healthy lifestyles within the setting
- providing children with a healthy balanced diet
- providing children with adequate exercise and outdoor activities
- promoting physical and mental well-being
- working in partnership with parents to ensure children are adequately supported with regard to adopting a healthy lifestyle
- ensuring that the health needs of children and young people with learning difficulties or disabilities are addressed.

How can childminders help children to stay safe?

The aims of this outcome are:

- to ensure that children and young people are safe from maltreatment, neglect, violence and sexual exploitation
- to ensure that children and young people are safe from accidental injury and death
- to ensure that children and young people are safe from bullying and discrimination
- to ensure that children have stability and are suitably cared for.

Helping children to stay safe is another essential part of a childminder's job. Adequate supervision for young children is paramount, while older children need to learn what constitutes danger and how to avoid unnecessary risks. Children need to be aware of how they can contribute to their own safety without being unduly frightened.

Issues of safety

In addition to ensuring that children are safe indoors and that the toys and equipment you provide are clean and suitable for the ages and stages of development of the children in your care, you will also need to think about issues such as:

- safety in the garden
- safety during planned outings
- safety travelling to and from school
- safety when collecting from school
- safety when parents are dropping off and collecting children from the setting
- safety online
- bullying
- stranger danger
- abuse.

All these areas need to be carefully considered and issues arising from them need to be addressed in order for you to ensure that children are kept safe at all times.

Putting rules in place for safety

Young children are very vulnerable and it is important that they are taught how to learn about the world around them in a safe and secure manner. Every childminding setting should have rules and boundaries in terms of behaviour in order to ensure the safety and comfort of everyone present.

You need to consider carefully your procedures for emergencies and evacuation. Make sure the children understand what they are to do in different situations, for example leaving the building in case of fire, etc.

It is essential that you are aware of and stick to the appropriate adult:child ratios at all times. You should never break this rule.

Ensuring the children in your care are safe

You can ensure the safety of the children in your care in a number of ways, such as:

- being vigilant at all times
- ensuring that the childminding premises, both inside and out, are free from potential risks
- ensuring that all toys and equipment are kept in a clean and good state of repair
- carrying out regular risk assessments
- actively observing the children in your care
- actively listening to the children in your care and responding appropriately; for example, sharing any concerns you may have with the appropriate people
- encouraging children to keep themselves safe by teaching them the importance of sticking to rules, assessing risks and making the right choices
- keeping abreast of any training opportunities suitable for the role of childminder

- ensuring that the children are aware of the potential risks to their safety and are taught how to deal with them

- ensuring that you are confident with dealing with issues of child protection

- ensuring that the needs of children with learning difficulties or disabilities are suitably addressed.

How can childminders help children to enjoy and achieve?

The aims of this outcome are:

- to ensure that children are ready for starting school

- to ensure that children enjoy school

- to ensure that children and young people achieve personal and social development and enjoy recreation.

Childminders must encourage children to develop the skills they will need for adulthood. Children have to understand how to get along with others in order to get the most out of life and its many varied experiences. First, children need to develop confidence when playing and learning, and childminders should nurture this aspect of children's development in order for them to enjoy the activities on offer and achieve their full potential.

Helping children achieve their potential

To help them achieve their full potential you need to look at what the children are good at and build on their interests in order to engage them enthusiastically in activities that will help to promote their all-round development.

Ensuring the children in your care enjoy and achieve

You can make sure that the children in your care enjoy and achieve by:

- ensuring that the provision is of an excellent standard

- ensuring that the children and young people are supported in their learning and play experiences
- ensuring that the provision promotes children's development and well-being and encourages them to meet early learning goals.

How can childminders help children to make a positive contribution?

The aims of this outcome are:

- to ensure that children and young people engage in decision-making and support the community and environment
- to ensure that children and young people are aware of how to behave in a positive manner both in and out of school
- to ensure that children and young people develop positive relationships and understand that bullying and discrimination is unacceptable
- to ensure that children and young people develop self-confidence and are encouraged to deal successfully with significant life changes and challenges.

For children to be able to make a positive contribution they need to develop a sense of belonging. This is possible if the childminder promotes and encourages self-respect and respect of others, so that the children learn to appreciate and respect the similarities and differences in others.

Supporting the children's development

It is important to work with the parents of the children you care for in order to meet each of the children's individual needs and to develop a satisfactory framework for managing the children's behaviour.

You can encourage the children in your care to gain a better understanding of the world they live in by providing appropriate activities and resources to enable them to explore.

Ensuring the children in your care make a positive contribution

You can help the children make a positive contribution by:

- supporting the children's development socially and emotionally
- supporting the children through significant life changes and encouraging them to make the right decisions
- providing the children with a framework for positive behaviour.

How can childminders help children to achieve economic well-being?

The aims of this outcome are:

- to ensure that all the children and young people have access to learning resources
- to ensure that the families are supported, regardless of their economic background.

Economic well-being is ensuring that no child is prevented from achieving their full potential due to economic disadvantage. Childminders need to be aware of the factors which may influence children's achievements and be sensitive to these factors.

Providing a welcoming environment

Childminders need to provide a welcoming environment and make sure that they are approachable in order to break down any barriers that may exist and enable the children to feel they belong in the setting.

All children learn in a warm and welcoming environment with knowledgeable adults they can trust and relate to, and it is important that childminders show an interest in each individual child and build on the relationship they have with them and their family.

Ensuring the children in your care achieve economic well-being

You can help the children in your care achieve economic well-being by:

- ensuring that children and young people are treated as individuals, regardless of their family background
- listening to and respecting the parents
- ensuring that the children are treated fairly
- ensuring that the children are included.

Chapter 9

Outstanding... Transitions to Primary School

Starting school is a huge milestone in every child's life and not one that should be looked on lightly. Even the most confident of children, who are clearly ready to embrace the challenges of a new setting and curriculum, may feel a little lost and in need of reassurance.

Starting school is inevitable and, although this is an exciting time in a child's life, it can bring with it some unrest and uncertainty, along with a little apprehension and sadness, when, having been such a large part of the family's life for so long, a child you may have been caring for since they were a baby, finally starts full-time education. The time they spend with you after this transition will be greatly reduced, if indeed they stay in your care at all.

As with all transitions in children's lives the secret to success is honesty. An outstanding childminder understands the importance of sharing information with both the children and their parents, so that they are all fully involved and aware of what to expect when the school term starts. Children will require sensitive support when moving from a familiar setting (your home) to new surroundings (school), but with your support they should be able to cope with the change and enjoy the new challenges ahead.

Although the majority of children will progress well when they begin their formal schooling, there is always the possibility that they may *regress*, if the changes to their usual routine and environment are too abrupt and therefore careful planning of the transition is necessary.

Helping children to make the transition

Important points to remember when supporting children who are about to start school are:

- **Ensure the children are the priority** – It is your job to ensure that the children's needs are met and respected and it is important that you involve the children in the whole process.

- **Explain what is happening** – Talk to the children and answer their questions honestly and openly. Explain the school routine and what they are likely to experience.

- **Be positive** – Even if your own experiences of school were not good, never allow yourself to be negative around the children. If they appear a little uncertain, then boost their confidence and explain to them how they will make new friends and experience many new challenges.

- **Share information with parents** – Always keep the parents informed of what is happening and answer their questions with honesty.

- **Access support from the school** – If you have been caring for the children during the school term, the chances are high that they will already have been to school with you on a regular basis when dropping off and collecting older children. This is invaluable for the children as they will already be familiar with the layout of the school and the teachers. This kind of familiarity will make the transition so much easier for the children. If possible, introduce the children to the teachers a few months before they are due to start and use the drop-off and collection time as an informal way of showing the children the classroom in more detail. It is a good idea to explain where coats are hung and where lunch boxes are stored, as well as pointing out some of the more interesting areas of the classroom such as the role-play and craft areas. Avoid giving the children too much information all at once as this can be quite daunting for them and always try to focus on the positive parts of the school day. Most schools will organise events prior to the new term where parents and children are invited into school to meet the teachers and get to know what happens in the school. This is an excellent way of putting both the parents' and children's mind at ease. Although you may well be taking children to school with you every day, it is important to remember that not all children will go to your local school. Parents are able to choose schools and, therefore, not all children will attend the school in their immediate catchment area. If this is the case, it will be more difficult for you to explain the set-up of the school as you may not be familiar with it yourself. In these circumstances you may need to contact the school and arrange a visit, or simply ask for clarification of certain facts so that you can relay these back to the children and their parents.

What to expect

So how difficult is it for children to make the transition to school and what should you, the childminder, expect?

Firstly, it is important to remember that all areas of children's development can be affected through transitions, particularly if the transition is unexpected such as the divorce or separation of the children's parents or a sudden bereavement. However, with starting school this transition is expected and anticipated and can, therefore, be planned for.

Many of the problems associated with the transition to school are about separation. Although it can be argued that a child who has been in day care from a young age has already experienced the separation from their parents, this can then shift to feelings of anxiety after being separated from their childminder. A young child who has, for example, spent half their week with their parents and the other half of the week with a childminder is no less likely to experience separation anxiety than a child who has always been with their parents.

As an outstanding childminder, you will understand this anxiety and recognise the importance of attachment and work hard to support the emotional well-being of the child during the period of transition to school. You may also be required to support the parents, who may be feeling guilty because they cannot escort their child to school on the first few days, and you will need to deal with these circumstances in a sensitive manner.

It is vital that you are aware of the effects that the transition to primary school can have on children and that you are aware of how to handle any situations. Always remember that children may not experience any adverse effects for some time and, just because all appears well for the first few weeks, you still need to be vigilant and be aware that sometimes children can take a number of weeks, or even months, for the realisation to set in that school is not a temporary change but one which they will need to accept for many years to come.

Possible effects

Effects on children through the transition to school may include:

- **Separation anxiety** – The children may become clingy and need constant reassurance from their parents or you. They may cry and beg you not to leave them. This can be very upsetting and you must not let the children see your own distress; instead comfort and reassure them.

- **Changes in behaviour** – The children may become angry or aggressive or, the total opposite, shy and introverted. Feelings of despair may overcome them as they find their way around their new surroundings. Again, you need to reassure them. Talk to the teacher and ask how they are getting on. If they have made new friends, then stay with them until a friend arrives so that you can be confident that they are with someone they know and like.

- **Tiredness** – The first few weeks of formal schooling can take their toll on young children and often they will be absolutely exhausted at the end of the day. Avoid asking them hundreds of questions about what they have done, no matter how tempting this may be, as quite often the children will be unwilling to answer as all they want to do is get back to your house and fall asleep!

The above are just a few of the common effects associated with children starting school. However, there are other, less common, effects that you also need to be aware of, such as regression, depression, lack of motivation, disorientation, etc. However, frequent chats with the class teacher and a close relationship with the children should reveal any major problems early on.

Completing transition forms

Ideally, all children who have been in some kind of registered childcare should have a transition form completed about them which is shared with the school. Settings with children who are in receipt of Nursery Education Funding are expected to complete a transition form which is sent to the children's school prior to their start date – this is a legal requirement. However, it is good practice and something that all outstanding child-minders should do for all children, regardless of whether you are in receipt of funding for them. Transition forms should be sent to the children's school by the first week of July. This form, along with the children's development file, will provide an invaluable insight into the children, their progress and their current stage of development, prior to them starting school. Below is an example of a transition form.

TRANSITION FORM

Name of child:

Date of birth:

Current setting: INSERT A PHOTOGRAPH

Entry date to current setting: OF THE CHILD HERE

Address of current setting:

Telephone number:

Key person:

Name of new school/setting:

Please indicate below any information shared

INFORMATION

	TICK HERE IF APPLICABLE		TICK HERE IF APPLICABLE
Observations/ Record of Achievement File		Look, Listen & Note Record	
Information provided by the parent (specify)		Individual Education Plans	
Looked-After child		CAF	

ADDITIONAL INFORMATION ENCLOSED (For children with SEN/Disability)

	TICK HERE IF APPLICABLE		TICK HERE IF APPLICABLE
Health Care Plans		Statutory Assessment Information	
Medical reports		Reports from outside agencies (please specify)	
IEP		Transition plan	
Other relevant information			

Signed .... Parent/carer
Signed .... Senco
Signed .... School to acknowledge receipt

The first page of the transition form should contain all the relevant information pertinent to the children, such as their personal details, and information about the setting they are currently attending.

The second page of the transition form (see the example below) should be completed by the children's parents or main carers.

YOUR CHILD

Tell us about your child: How does your child feel about moving to school?   What does your child enjoy doing?   Do they have any specific likes or dislikes?
Things we need to know about your child: Does your child have any allergies we need to be aware of?   What can your child eat/not eat?   Does your child have any medical conditions?

YOUR FAMILY/CARERS

Who does your family consist of?
Are there any other children who are important to your child?
What language is spoken at home?
Do you have any other information you would like to share with us?

The third page of the transition form should be completed by the child-minder and it gives a summative statement at the point of transition.

SUMMATIVE STATEMENT

What are the child's strengths?
What are the child's key areas of interest?
Has the child needed any support in specific areas of development? If yes, please explain how you have been supporting them.
How does the child feel about moving to school?

The final part of the transition form is the Early Years Foundation Stage Tracker Sheet and this shows a summary statement of the child's development at the point of transition. Tracking sheets can be set out in a variety of ways and, providing all the relevant information is included, it does not really matter how the sheets are developed. There is an example of a tracker sheet on the following page.

If you are a childminder who is caring for a child who has been identified as having additional needs, then it will be necessary for a transition plan to be completed. Your local early years consultant or childcare inclusion officer will be able to assist with the completion of a transition plan should this be necessary.

Occasionally, you may find that parents are un-cooperative and it may be difficult to get them to complete the forms. Parental engagement is key to outstanding practice and it is, therefore, vital that you do your utmost to build meaningful relationships with the parents of the children in your care.

EYFS TRACKER SHEET

Name of child:			Date of birth:				
Name of setting:			Key worker:				

Area of Learning							
Phase							
Birth–11 mths							
8–20 mths							
16–26 mths							
22–36 mths							
30–50 mths							
40–60+ mths							

DATE ....

Always bear in mind that some parents are not familiar with filling in forms and they may require a little support. It is perfectly acceptable for you to support a parent when they are completing the parent/carer section of the transition form.

Chapter 10
Outstanding...
Self-evaluation and
Continual Professional
Development

Although not compulsory, Ofsted recommends that all practitioners regularly complete a self-evaluation form (SEF). The SEF can be found on Ofsted's website and it is an excellent way of providing evidence that you think about your practice and consider ways of evaluating and improving the service that you provide. If you choose not to complete a SEF, then you will need to provide alternative evidence for the inspector's visit to show that you are confident and capable of carrying out self-evaluation.

Self-evaluation is essential if you are to achieve and retain an outstanding grade. No provider is perfect and all childminders are learning all the time. Everyone makes mistakes; however, it is how you learn from these mistakes and move forward that is important and makes you outstanding.

The self-evaluation form

The SEF was revamped in September 2012 and made more user-friendly. The SEF is designed to help the provider to review and improve their provision and it is important to remember that, even when you have achieved an outstanding grade, in order to ensure that you stay there, you will need to continually review and improve your practice. Completing the SEF initially is quite time-consuming and you will be asked to provide evidence of how you carry out certain aspects of your work, such as:

- *What are the views of the children and their parents or carers? How do you know what their views are? Please give examples of any action you have taken to change your provision as a result of their views.* You will need to show how you carry out questionnaires and request feedback from children and parents, and how you use the information you receive.

- *On the basis of your evaluation, what are your priorities for improvement?* You will need to explain how you have used the information provided by the children and parents to carry out any improvements or changes. You will need to show that you are able to prioritise and show how you do this.

- *How well does the setting meet the needs of children in the Early Years Foundation Stage?* For this you will need to share information regarding observations and assessments in addition to relevant training.

The SEF also covers important areas such as safeguarding, equality and diversity, healthy lifestyles and making a positive contribution, and an excellent knowledge of the EYFS framework will help with these areas along with evidence of effective policies and procedures and up-to-date training.

Once you have completed the SEF initially, it is just a means of updating as and when necessary. Although Ofsted do not state when the SEF should be updated, it is good practice to review it regularly and certainly you should be updating it at least once a year and when any changes have been implemented, such as employing or changing any assistants you work with or making any changes to the environment in which you work.

The advantages of completing the SEF

Putting aside the time you will need to spend on the SEF, it is important not to dwell too long on the disadvantages but to look closely at the advantages of completing the self-evaluation form. It will enable you to:

- keep track of any changes you have implemented and how effective these have been

- evaluate the impact of the service you provide and how this affects the welfare, learning and development of the children in your care

- prepare for your inspection

- provide evidence to Ofsted that you are confident in how to carry out self-evaluation

- show you are committed to your job

- provide detailed information for the inspector, prior to your inspection, of what works well in your setting and what you personally think you need to improve.

Completing the SEF

The SEF asks you to *evaluate* your own practice and you will be asked to 'grade' your own provision in a similar way to how the inspectors themselves will grade you. If you grade yourself as being outstanding, be sure to have the evidence in place to support this claim!

In order to complete the self-evaluation form online, Ofsted will issue you with a unique password known as an Ofsted Security Token (OST). Full instructions on how to complete the SEF can be found on the Ofsted website. If you prefer to complete the form by hand, then you can download the relevant document from the website; when completed it needs to be posted to Ofsted.

Continuing professional development

Continuing professional development, or CPD as it is often referred to, is the means by which professionals such as yourself *maintain* their knowledge and skills relating to their professional status. Although you will probably think about training as and when you feel it is necessary, it is good practice and essential for all outstanding childminders to recognise the importance of CPD and to put in place a clearly defined and structured approach to your learning, in order to ensure that you are competent and highly skilled to carry out the tasks involved with caring for children and that your knowledge and practical experience is of the highest possible level.

Childminding not only demands a love for working with children – it also requires a sound knowledge of them and therefore it is vital that all childminders access training and are committed to developing their skills and understanding on a long-term basis. Achieving a level three Diploma in childcare, although worthy and respectable, does not mean that your training is complete and you may like to consider a whole range of further qualifications such as a Foundation Degree in Early Years, Early Years Professional Status, or even an Honours Degree – there is absolutely nothing to stop you from accessing training to the full and it will show parents, colleagues and Ofsted that you are committed to your role.

Planning for CPD

In order to competently plan for CPD, it is a good idea to jot down on paper your existing skills and the areas you feel you could improve on. This will help you to focus on future training and identify any gaps you feel are lacking in your current knowledge.

A simple list such as the one in the example below should help you to quickly identify which areas you feel you can improve on.

AREAS OF IMPROVEMENT

- Are my communication skills good? Can I improve on them?

- Am I well organised? Can I improve on my organisation skills?

- Am I fully aware of the EYFS and what it entails?

- Do I understand how children learn and develop?

- Am I confident observing and assessing children?

- Am I capable of planning for children's future development?

- Do I understand how to ensure that I keep children healthy?

- Do I understand how to ensure that I keep children safe?

- Do I know how to report suspected abuse?

- Do I know how to respond if I have any concerns about a child?

It is hoped, as you are looking to become an outstanding childminder, that you can confidently answer 'yes' to most of the questions posed in the example. However, if you are in any doubt then you should be seeking additional training. Safeguarding, for example, is a very important subject and one that most people prefer not to discuss. There is the fear of not knowing what to do should a child disclose information to you and the reluctance of acting on what has been said in case you are wrong.

Creating a professional development plan

You may find it helpful to produce a professional development plan like the one shown in the example on the following page. A PDP can be updated regularly, as and when you consider it necessary, and it should include both short- and long-term goals. Short-term goals should show the areas you wish to develop within say, six to 12 months, and long-term goals should show where you see yourself in two to five years' time. Obviously things will change which is why the plan can and should be adapted.

When developing a professional development plan it is vital that you are not over-ambitious, as this can put a huge dent in your confidence when you review your plan and find that you have not managed to achieve your targets. The key to a successful development plan is to:

- identify the areas you need to develop
- decide how you are going to go about achieving your goal; for example, enrol on a training course, attend an open day, etc.
- set a target date to achieve your objective – this may be dependent on the length and start date of a particular course.

Always make sure that your plan is realistic – start with one or two important areas you need to develop and move on from there. If you begin with over-enthusiasm and enrol on a dozen courses, all with an achievement date of six months, you are going to set yourself up to fail. Be realistic and set a well-thought-out time frame in which to achieve your objectives. Three well-thought-out objectives with a realistic timescale for achievement of, say, two years is much better than attempting to change six areas of development in 12 months and failing miserably. Not only will your confidence take a knock, you will be absolutely exhausted and end up achieving nothing and enjoying even less!

PROFESSIONAL DEVELOPMENT PLAN

DATE PLAN WAS LAST MODIFIED:

DATE PLAN WILL BE REVIEWED:

Description of Current Position:

SHORT-TERM GOALS

Areas I would like to develop	Why I consider it necessary to develop these areas	Actions	Deadline
1.			
2.			
3.			

LONG-TERM GOALS

Areas I would like to develop	Why I consider it necessary to develop these areas	Actions	Deadline
1.			
2.			
3.			

Setting personal objectives

It is often much harder for childminders to identify their personal objectives as they do not usually have colleagues to discuss things with and therefore it is very important that you are honest with yourself. Do not pretend that you are confident and up to date with a certain aspect of training just because it does not particularly appeal to you, as, chances are, this is the area you are most likely to need to address. When planning your PDP you need to seriously consider the following points:

- your existing skills
- your existing experience
- the ages and development of the children you are currently working with
- the needs of the children/families you are currently working with
- any existing problems or areas of concern in your current practice which you have identified
- any changes in your role
- any requirements to update existing qualifications which have expired, such as first aid or child protection.

Developing a personal portfolio

Before starting your PDP it is a good idea to build up a personal portfolio of your existing qualifications and experience. This portfolio is useful to show to parents and to Ofsted and keeps all your certificates together. Your portfolio could contain anything which shows how you are a professional practitioner and will probably include:

- a current CV
- certificates from school, college, etc. – these should be in date order and do not have to relate to childcare
- first-aid certificate – your certificate may be nearing renewal and, therefore, this could be one of the areas of development you add to your PDP
- references from parents or past employers
- any relevant college assignments.

Chapter 11
Outstanding... Inspections

Many childminders, and indeed schoolteachers, dread their routine inspection by Ofsted. Having an Ofsted inspector or inspectors come into your home to assess and grade the work you do can be nerve-racking even for experienced, confident childminders who have dozens of qualifications and are at the top of their profession. Therefore, it is understandable that childminders with only a few years' experience and limited training may feel out of their depth when their inspection is looming.

The inspector – friend or foe?

The important thing to remember is that the inspector is *not your enemy!* Armed with a laptop and endless questions, you may feel the inspector is here to interrogate and reprimand but the opposite is actually the case. The inspector, like you, has a job to do and their job is to provide regular checks to ensure that all registered childminders are continuing to meet appropriate standards of day care. The inspector should not be regarded as someone out to 'trip you up' or 'catch you out' and these negative feelings will only leave you feeling more ill at ease if you allow them to surface. An outstanding childminder recognises the need for their provision to be inspected and rises to the challenge!

If you are following the recommended procedures for childminding and are up to date with all your essential paperwork (see Chapter Five), then you should have nothing to worry about and little preparation from you for the inspection should be required.

What to expect from your inspection

Registration and inspections used to be carried out by the local authority. However, in 2001 this was transferred to the Ofsted directorate. It is the job of Ofsted inspectors to look at, and monitor, the ways in which childcare providers demonstrate how they meet the necessary criteria.

The Childcare Act 2006 brought about new changes as it set out how Early Years provision must be registered and introduced the EYFS as the statutory framework for the education and welfare of children from birth to the 31 August following their fifth birthday.

From September 2008, the EYFS formed the basis of inspections of provision for young children and the introduction of this framework allowed Ofsted the opportunity of bringing greater consistency to the inspection of Early Years provision across the sector.

From September 2012, Ofsted introduced a new inspection framework which focused more on interactions with children and less on paperwork and this was a welcome relief to many practitioners who were beginning to see their role as being predominantly paper based with less and less time to spend with the children. Although the necessary paperwork is still essential, childcare practices and observations of activities which put emphasis on children's development in the areas of learning are the main focus of inspections under the new framework.

Ofsted has the power to investigate your setting as a childminder to ensure that you are meeting the appropriate standards and can request that changes are made if necessary. Ofsted also has the power to terminate your registration, if your setting does not conform to the appropriate standards.

Newly registered childminders will usually have their first Ofsted inspection within a short period of time after their registration. After the initial inspection Ofsted will usually carry out further inspections at least once every three years. However, in certain circumstances, as listed below, inspections will be more frequent.

- If the last inspection concluded that the quality of childcare you provide had significant weaknesses.

- If there have been significant changes to the setting since the last inspection, such as a change of premises.

- If a complaint has been made against you that suggests you are not meeting the appropriate standards or providing adequate care for the children.

Ofsted will not usually give any notice of an Early Years inspection. However, in some circumstances, they may telephone beforehand to ensure that you are available and that the inspector's visit will not be a wasted one. Ofsted recognises that childminders, unlike other providers, are often out and about, taking children to and from school or attending toddler groups, support groups, etc., and it is in everyone's interests to ensure that the inspection date is convenient and that the childminder will be at home on the date of the planned inspection.

During an inspection the inspector will begin by explaining how the inspection will be carried out and detailing their own role in the process. The inspector will recognise that, despite having your inspection, you also have children to care for and a routine to adhere to and they will set aside a suitable time to talk to you and give feedback.

It is perfectly natural to feel a little nervous about your inspection, particularly if you are a newly qualified childminder and have had little or no experience in dealing with childcare inspections. Even very experienced childminders still feel a little apprehensive about the inspection; after all, someone is coming into your home to inspect and grade a service you are providing, and you will be striving to achieve the best grading possible – outstanding!

When an inspector arrives at your home, check their ID *before* allowing them access! This will not antagonise the inspector; it will show that you are sincere about the safety of the children in your care and that you are aware of the correct procedure regarding access to strangers while carrying out your childminding duties. If the inspector cannot show you any ID, or you are in any doubt whatsoever about who they say they are, then leave them on the doorstep while you clarify the situation with your Ofsted regional office.

It is important to carry on your normal routine without making any changes. Disruption should be kept to a minimum; although, of course, you will need to be available to talk with the inspector when required.

In order to carry out the inspection, the inspector will need to gather evidence about the quality and standards of your provision and this will probably be done by:

- observing what the children and adults in the setting are doing

- talking to the children and, if possible, the parents to find out their views on the childcare provided. It is a good idea to request some or all of the parents to complete questionnaires prior to your inspection, giving their ideas and opinions of the service you provide, if they cannot be present in person during the inspection. This will enable the inspector to have an idea of how your service is viewed by the parents of the children you care for

- checking your premises and equipment to ensure that they are safe and suitable and how well they are used to promote the outcomes for the children

- checking your written records, procedures and any other necessary documentation.

Throughout the inspection the inspector will make notes. When the inspection is complete, usually after about two hours, the inspector will let you know the outcome of their findings. You will normally see a display of the inspector's judgments on a laptop computer and it is these judgments which will be included in your final report. At this point you may correct factual information or ask for further clarification of any of the points the inspector raises.

The report and grading

After the inspection the inspector will write a short report which will include information such as:

- the grade you are being given after the inspection
- a summary of how well you manage your provision
- a summary of the quality of the service you provide
- a summary of how well you support the children in your care
- a summary of how you have improved since your last inspection and whether any suggested improvements have been implemented, if appropriate
- any recommendations the inspector deems necessary in order to improve your current provision.

The inspector will also give details about whether you comply with the Early Years Register requirements.

After your inspection you will be sent an Inspection report. If there are any factual errors in the report at this stage, you must inform Ofsted immediately as the report will be published on the internet shortly afterwards. The report, when published on the internet, will not include your name or your full address.

Ofsted inspectors use a four-point grading scale to make judgments on childcare settings and this is set out below:

- **GRADE 1 – Outstanding** – This shows an exceptional provider whose provision is above the normal standard. The provision is seen as benefitting children and preparing them for their next stage of learning.

- **GRADE 2 – Good** – This shows a strong provider where the outcomes for children are firmly established.

- **GRADE 3 – Satisfactory** – This shows a provider whose practice requires improvement. This grading will be replaced in November in line with schools and colleges. Satisfactory will then be known as 'Requires Improvement'

- **GRADE 4 – Inadequate** – This grade has two categories:

Category 1 – This shows a weak provider who gives cause for concern. The inspector deems this kind of provision to be capable of improving *without* external support.

Category 2 – This shows a poor provider who is in urgent need of attention. The inspector deems this kind of provision as being unlikely to improve and external support is required. It is likely that the inspector will recommend enforcement action for a provider deemed Grade 4, category 2.

What happens next?

If your childcare provision is judged as 'requires improvement' or 'good', the report will include recommendations to help you to improve your provision further. The inspector will check whether these recommendations have been implemented at your next inspection (within three years from the date of your last inspection). However, if the inspector considers that the quality of care you are providing is inadequate then it will be because you are failing to meet the necessary criteria. If this judgment is made Ofsted will either:

- Send you a letter to tell you what action you must take to improve the care you provide. This letter is called a *notice of action to improve*. You will be required to let Ofsted know when you have taken the necessary action and an announced or unannounced visit may be made to check that the necessary improvements have been made. If you ignore the notice of action or the improvements you make have little impact on the outcome of your childcare provision, then Ofsted may take further enforcement measures. You will receive a further inspection within six to 12 months of your initial visit.

- If your childcare provision is classed as poor and is considered in need of immediate improvement, then Ofsted will take enforcement action such as issuing you with a *compliance notice*. An inspector will follow this notice up to ensure that the improvements have been made. In rare cases Ofsted may consider *suspending* or *cancelling* your registration. If Ofsted consider it necessary to take serious action against your setting but still allow your registration to continue, then they will inspect your premises again, either at the date given on any enforcement action or within three to six months, whichever is the sooner.

How to impress the inspector

Preparation is a key factor when anticipating your forthcoming inspection. No one can accurately guess exactly what will happen during an inspection; this will depend entirely on the day the inspection takes place and which children you are caring for at the time. Even how the children are feeling on that particular day can have an impact on the way your inspection may go. If one of the children in your care is feeling a bit off-colour or tired or simply refusing to cooperate, it may add to the stress you are already feeling. The important thing to remember is that the inspector understands that children rarely do exactly what they are expected to and it is how you *handle* any awkward or difficult situations that will be looked at. Try to relax and act as normally as possible. Go about your daily routines as you usually would and avoid making changes that would confuse or disrupt the children's usual patterns. After all, if you are complying with the requirements set out by

Ofsted and are working within the set criteria *all of the time,* which is what you should be doing, then you really have little to worry about.

Although you will be striving to achieve an 'outstanding' grade for your business, it is important to remember that the inspector is looking at how you run your business *all* of the time and not just for the hours they are present. Therefore, striving to overly impress is unnecessary and will come across as false.

By taking the inspector on a brief tour of your premises and pointing out how you have made each of the areas safe, hygienic and suitable for the children will help you to answer many of the questions the inspector will inevitably raise and you will be able to elaborate on the facilities you have available.

Think carefully about each of the important points the inspector may ask and use each area of your premises to satisfy them that you are aware of, and concerned with, the aspects in question. For example:

- Hygienic work practices could be discussed when showing the inspector your bathroom, toilet and nappy changing facilities.

- Safety could be discussed in the playroom and outdoor areas.

- Dietary needs, hygiene and healthy eating could be discussed in the kitchen.

- Learning and development could be discussed when showing the inspector the activities, resources and experiences you provide.

These are just a few of the many ways you can provide evidence of your working practice.

Making sure you are ready

There are a number of other points which you should consider to make sure you are ready for your inspection and these are listed below.

- Ensure that you and any assistants or other childminders you work with are familiar with all the relevant documents needed for running a childminding business; for example, the EYFS framework, which changed in September 2012.

- Ensure that you have put right any weaknesses identified in your last inspection report, if applicable.

- Ensure that you have completed the self-evaluation form (see Chapter Ten).

- Ensure that you have all the required records which the inspector will need to see, such as contracts, attendance register, etc.

- Keep any information about how parents view your service and any improvements you have made as a result. It is a good idea to produce a simple questionnaire to give to parents, prior to your inspection or periodically, say once a year, to establish how the parents of the children you care for view your setting and the childcare provision you provide. Often constructive criticism can be very helpful and everyone responds well to praise! On the next page is an example of a questionnaire you might like to use or adapt.

- Ensure that you have available any records you keep of complaints about the childcare you provide.

- Ensure that you have notified Ofsted of any significant changes you have made to your provision, for example any changes to the premises or people employed to look after the children.

The questionnaire on the next page can be adapted to suit your own childcare setting and it may be a good idea to distribute these periodically, especially if you have got new children starting. A good time to give a questionnaire out may be just prior to renewing a contract, so that any changes implemented can be reflected in the contract and you can be sure that the service you provide is the right one for the family.

Keeping the children entertained during your inspection

It has to be said that the children themselves will have a lot to do with the way your inspection goes! If you are caring for a child who often resorts to temper tantrums, sulks or has difficulty cooperating, then don't make the mistake of thinking that they will be on their best behaviour because there is a stranger present – this will simply not happen! In fact, often the reverse may be true as they strive to push the boundaries even further to see if they can get away with anything more while someone new is in the setting.

QUESTIONNAIRE FOR PARENTS

In order that I can continue to provide a good quality childcare service that benefits all the children and their parents, I would be much obliged if you would kindly take the time to complete this short questionnaire and return it to me as soon as possible.

1 Are you happy with the overall childcare I provide for your child/children?

2 If there are any improvements you feel I could make which would be of benefit to you, what would these be?

3 Are the hours I am available to work acceptable to you?

4 Are you happy with the meals I provide? Do you have any suggestions for improvements?

5 Are you happy with the activities I provide for your child/children? Do you think these could be improved in any way?

6 Do you consider that your child is happy in my setting and are there any ways I could make their time with me more enjoyable?

7 If your child/children are of school age, do you consider that they get sufficient help from me with regard to their homework/studies? Can you suggest any improvement?

8 Are you happy with the information I provide with regard to your child's daily routines? Is there any further information you would like?

9 Are there any further comments you would like to make which may help me to continually strive to improve my day care and before- and after-school service, in order that all the children in my care remain happy and secure?

The key here is to be prepared. Unless you have only just begun to care for a child, you should have a good idea of what makes them 'tick' – their likes and dislikes and what triggers unacceptable behaviour, and it is paramount that you are prepared for all eventualities. One of the reasons why you should not change your usual routine is so that you do not upset or confuse children who rely on the daily structure for security. Therefore, if you usually serve a snack at 10am, do not put this off because the inspector is present – rest assured most children will ask for it! If a child usually has a nap at a set time, then make sure you keep to this routine to avoid the child becoming overtired, which often results in unacceptable behaviour which will, of course, add to your problems.

It is important to focus on the aspects which are important during your inspection and this does *not* include entertaining the inspector! Your job is to care for the children. Although you will be expected to provide information and answer questions, this has to be done *while* you are carrying out your duties and not *instead* of them.

Be aware, at all times, how the children are behaving and how they are responding to the activities you have provided. You should have a good idea of the level of concentration the children have and the stage of development they are at and it is unrealistic to expect a child of two to sit at a table with a jigsaw puzzle for two hours while you give the inspector a tour of your home. Involve the children as much as possible during the inspection and show the inspector how the children respond to you. Ask one of the children to show the inspector where they hang their coat and bag, where the potty is kept, how they help set the table for lunch or help with simple tasks. This will both occupy the child and show the inspector how you involve the children in the day-to-day routines.

Change the activities you provide regularly and, as soon as the children appear bored or distracted, introduce something new for them to do. Your experience of caring for children should help you to know which activities are enjoyed the most by the children, and often painting, play-dough modelling, junk modelling and stories are effective.

Planning is a vital part of a childminder's job and never is this more evident than during inspections. If you plan your work effectively a visit from an inspector should not throw your day into chaos, as you should already know what you are hoping to do with the children during that particular day and should not, therefore, be frantically scouring the cupboard for a bald paintbrush or dried-out play dough. This is a sure sign that your daily activities are unplanned or even non-existent and may lead the inspector to believe that you provide little opportunity for the children to play and learn. As you have bought this book and clearly want to become an outstanding childminder, I would be very surprised if this was the case in your setting!

Chapter 12
Outstanding...
Becoming Outstanding and Staying Outstanding

Outstanding? What next?

You've done it! The feeling of smug satisfaction and utter relief washes over you as you close the door on the Ofsted inspector who has completed a thorough examination of your premises, facilities, resources, records, routines, in fact just about everything, and come to the conclusion that you are providing an 'outstanding' service. Congratulations! Pat yourself on the back, for you have achieved something worthwhile. All your hard work has paid off and been recognised and you can look forward to receiving your 'outstanding' certificate to display on your wall along with your inspection report to share with parents.

But what happens next? Satisfaction you may well feel, and quite rightly so; but there is no place for complacency in this profession. Achieving an outstanding award is one thing, maintaining it is quite another and, if you wish to remain at the top of the ladder as far as providing an exceptional childcare service is concerned, you will need to keep up with changes, attend training classes and *evaluate* your methods and your practice regularly. Now is not the time to sit back and let things slip, secure in the knowledge that you will have no more inspections for three years. Now is the time to reflect on the inspection and think about the areas you feel impressed the inspector – the feedback you were given should help you to ascertain this – and which areas you think you could improve upon. While everything the inspector has said to you is fresh in your mind, it is a good idea to make a few notes and jot down the things you were particularly pleased with and those you feel you should act upon. If you have received an outstanding result, then the inspector will feel that you are running an exceptional setting which has excellent outcomes for the children and, as such, the inspector will not have found any major issues they are not happy with. However, this does not mean that you cannot *improve* and *build upon* the provision you are currently providing in order to maintain your outstanding service, and it is likely that the feedback provided by the inspector will highlight these areas. *No one* is perfect and all childminders, even those with an outstanding report, should be looking at ways in which they can add to their knowledge, reflect upon their practice and develop their skills in order to go from strength to strength.

It is a good idea to share your achievement with the parents of the children you are caring for and you should furnish them with a copy of your Inspection report, perhaps inviting them to comment on the content and share their own opinions with you.

By achieving an outstanding Inspection report you will have demonstrated to the Ofsted inspector that your setting is highly effective in making sure that children learn through an enjoyable range of stimulating experiences in a setting which is exemplary. You will have successfully shown that you understand how children learn and develop and demonstrated a sound knowledge of supporting the children in your care in reaching achievable targets and building self-esteem and confidence.

In order to gain an outstanding grade, you will need to have shown that you are well informed with regard to the needs of the children and show that you have a good understanding of the importance of discussing children's progress with parents and carers and maintaining accurate written records of the children's progress and achievements.

Reflecting on practice

Unless this is your first Ofsted inspection, it is likely that your previous report highlighted points which the inspector felt, at that time, you could improve upon and, if this is the case, you will need to address these points in order to achieve the outstanding outcome you require. By acting on any recommendations made by the inspector, you will be demonstrating a willingness and understanding of how to evaluate yourself and your practice, make any necessary changes and put these changes into effect. Typically some of the ways in which Ofsted inspectors identify ways in which providers could further improve their practice by helping the children in their care to enjoy their learning and achieve well include suggesting:

- increasing the adult interaction with the children

- extending the children's imaginative play, outdoor learning and experiences for children attending the setting before and after school

- improving the balance between supervised and creative free play

- developing the use of questioning to extend children's learning – this could be achieved by asking 'open-ended' questions which encourage the child to think about their answer and give in-depth answers rather than simple 'yes' or 'no' responses.

So, how can you successfully evaluate your setting and build on and improve your existing knowledge?

In many cases it is often easier to improve your practice when you can clearly see where improvements are needed. However, a childminder with an outstanding Ofsted inspection report could be forgiven for believing that they need not make any changes or improvements to their practice as they are already 'perfect'. This is, of course, an inaccurate assumption and *all* childminders, whatever their grading can and indeed should be striving to improve their practice all the time. By evaluating your business and being a reflective practitioner, you will be able to recognise your good points and strengths and identify those areas which you feel you could improve upon. All childminders will have at least one area of their practice which they feel they could gain additional knowledge about. This may be learning to be more assertive, or gaining more information with regard to safeguarding children against abuse and, in these cases, it would be beneficial for the childminder to look at enrolling on suitable training to advance their knowledge in the areas they feel are slightly lacking.

You may decide that the time is right for you to further your qualifications and a Quality Assurance Programme or Foundation Degree course could be suitable for you.

In order to continually improve the service you provide it is important that you reflect *often* on the work that you do, rather than occasionally spare a little time to give out questionnaires to the parents of the children you are caring for, perhaps because you have an inspection looming and feel this is something you *should* be doing. Reflecting on your work is something you *must* do in order to continue improving and moving forward.

Being a reflective practitioner is not simply being able to take on criticism and turn it into something positive, although this is certainly a part of it. The true meaning of being a reflective practitioner is to be able to look at yourself and your practice honestly and openly, to recognise where changes are necessary and to bring these changes about successfully. To do this, you need to ask yourself some important questions and answer them *honestly*:

- Which areas of my practice are the strongest?
- Which areas of my practice are the weakest?
- How do I know this? What evidence do I have to back up these assumptions?
- What complaints or suggestions have I received from parents in the past six months?
- How have I responded to these comments or suggestions?
- Was my response adequate?
- How can I access further training which I feel would be beneficial to my business?
- Do I feel prepared for all eventualities?
- Can I accommodate the wishes of all the children and their families adequately?

Of course, one of the easiest ways of ensuring that you are meeting the needs of the children and their families is to ask them. Parents are usually forthcoming with suggestions and, if you ask them if they are happy with the service you are providing or if there are any areas they feel you could improve upon, they are often happy to discuss matters with you. Older children can, of course, be asked for their own opinions on the facilities and activities you provide. Try enlisting their help with planning and ask them which activities and toys they would like you to provide. It is important, however, once you have sought the opinions of parents and children, that you take their comments on board and do your best to accommodate their wishes. You should explain along the way anything which you feel it is not possible for you to comply with so that no one feels their suggestions have been disregarded or ignored.

Further reading and resources

Organisations

British Association for the Study and Prevention of Child Abuse and Neglect
17 Priory Street
York
North Yorkshire
YO1 6ET
www.baspcan.org.uk

British Nutrition Foundation (BNF)
Imperial House 6th Floor 15–19 Kingsway
London
WC2B 6UN
www.nutrition.org.uk

British Red Cross
44 Moorfields
London
EC2Y 9AL
www.redcross.org.uk

Child Accident Prevention Trust (CAPT)
Canterbury Court
1–3 Brixton Road
London
SW9 6DE
www.capt.org.uk

Kidscape
2 Grosvenor Gardens
London
SW1W 0DH
www.kidscape.org.uk

Professional Association for Childcare and Early Years (PACEY)
Royal Court
81 Tweedy Road
Bromley
Kent
BR1 1TG
www.pacey.org.uk

National Society for the Prevention of Cruelty to Children (NSPCC)
Weston House
42 Curtain Road
London
EC2A 3NH
www.nspcc.org.uk

Parenting NI
Andras House
60 Great Victoria Street
Belfast
BT2 7BB
www.parentingni.org

Royal Society for the Prevention of Accidents (RoSPA)
RoSPA House
28 Calthorpe Road
Edgbaston
Birmingham
B15 1RP
www.rospa.com

Websites

Department for Education (DfE)
www.education.gov.uk

Food Standards Agency
www.food.gov.uk

Ofsted
www.ofsted.gov.uk

Books

Childminder's Handbook, Allison Lee
Childminder's Guide to Play and Activities, Allison Lee
The Inside Guide to Being a Childminder, Allison Lee
Childminder's Guide to Health and Safety and Child Protection, Allison Lee
Childminder's Guide to Child Development, Allison Lee

Index

OTHER TITLES IN THIS SERIES:

How to be an Outstanding Primary School Teacher
by David Dunn

OTHER TITLES AVAILABLE FROM BLOOMSBURY
EDUCATION:

100 Ideas for Early Years Practitioners: Outstanding Practice
by Lucy Peet
100 Ideas for Early Years Practitioners: School Readiness
by Clare Ford
Breaking Through Barriers to Boys' Achievement
by Gary Wilson

How to be an Outstanding Childminder

M ω